THE WISDOM OF EVE

BY **MARY ORR**

★ Revised Edition

★

DRAMATISTS
PLAY SERVICE
INC.

THE WISDOM OF EVE was first produced by Gryphon Theatricals, Inc., at the Three Muses Theatre, New York City, on March 9, 1979. It was directed by Frank Biancamano; the set design was by Ron Kron; the costume design was by Sandy Handloser; the lighting design was by Sylvia Yoshioka. The cast was as follows:

KAREN ROBERTS	Maryellen Flynn
EVE HARRINGTON	Nancy Weems
MARGO CRANE	Diane de Lorian
CLEMENT HOWELL	John McComb
LLOYD ROBERTS	John Corey
HARVEY	Gary Pollard
JACK MARSHALL	Sal Carollo
TALLY-HO THOMPSON	Tom McGreevey
BERT HINKLE	Derek Steeley
VERA FRANKLIN	Angela Christi

CHARACTERS

(in order of importance)

EVE, a theatre fan
KAREN, an ex-actress
MARGO, a famous star
LLOYD, a playwright, Karen's husband
CLEMENT, Margo's husband and producer
HARVEY, Margo's stage manager
"TALLY-HO" THOMPSON, a newspaper columnist
BERT HINKLE, a theatrical agent
LEILA, Margo's maid
VERA FRANKLIN, a young actress

SETTING

The scene is in and around a New York Theater, a country house, a New York apartment, etc.

Time is unfortunately the present.

SETTING

A simple permanent set should serve for the fluid action of this play. It may be modified or elaborated, according to the individual taste of the director or the financial capacity of the producing company.

Downstage right is a canvas flat with a door in it, slightly raked towards the audience. This door is narrow and broken-down looking and is surrounded by dirty, grey brick. It suggests the average stage door of a Broadway theatre. Downstage left is another door in another slanted flat. This is smartly painted in green and framed by a vine-colored trellis. It suggests the side door of a country house leading out to the garden. Between these two flats, slightly raised, are the two small sets. In front of them is empty space.

Margo Crane's theatrical dressing room at the Circle Theatre is revealed when the lights are lit on the stage right side. Karen's library is on the other side, either lit or in darkness, depending on the action.

(See Diagram)

Note for the Director: The acting should be allowed to spill over into the downstage area when either of these rooms is in use. When one room is lit and the other not in use, it is blacked out by the lights.

The action of the play takes place over two theatrical seasons. These may occur in any years from the present day onward.

No particular date is emphasized.

THE WISDOM OF EVE

ACT ONE

When the house lights dim, the stage is in darkness. Mysteriously, as if out of nowhere, a circular pool of light picks out Karen Roberts, who is standing down near the footlights in the center.

Karen is a chic blonde in her fifties. She is wearing a mink coat, a scarf over her hair, and she carries an umbrella.

KAREN.   Ladies and gentlemen, I'm Mrs. Lloyd Roberts. Before I married I was an actress. My stage name was Karen Anders. I wasn't very successful. Oh, I had talent, but talent is not enough to make you a star. You need other qualities.... Tonight I'm going to tell you about a girl who *does* have these qualities. Her name is Eve Harrington.

It was nearly two years ago when I spoke to Eve˙ for the first time. She was standing at the stage door of the Circle Theatre waiting for Margo Crane to come out. Margo is not only a tremendous force in the theatre, she is my best friend. She has been the star in three of my husband's smash hits. My husband, you will gather, is a playwright ... Margo is marvelous. A dream, when she's not being a nightmare. Like all stars she is surrounded by satellites. Eve Harrington used to be one of them — an autograph hound, a nobody. When I first saw her she was just a little ghost haunting the shadows of a dark alley ... *(She gestures towards the right by the footlights.)* Picture over in that corner the stage door of the Circle Theatre. It's at the end of a long, dark passage. No one would dare to venture down it but actors, who are never afraid of anything — except dramatic critics. It was one of those misty November evenings when the elements were undecided. To rain or not to rain. So, since a faint drizzle was dampening the alley, Margo's fans had not appeared at the stage door in their usual numbers. In fact, there was only one. Eve Harrington!... *(During the last sentences, she opens her umbrella and walks across to the R. of the stage. As she does so, the spotlight in which she has been standing fades out and a faint pool of light reveals the R. corner of the stage. All we see in the way of scenery is the "flat" with a narrow door in it on which the words STAGE ENTRANCE are printed. Standing in front of the door, we see Eve. She is dressed in a little red coat. The collar is turned up. Her hair is in strings and she looks like a bedraggled mouse. As Karen pauses to lower her umbrella, Eve steps forward and touches her arm.)*

EVE.   Mrs. Roberts ...

KAREN.   Yes, what is it?

EVE.   Forgive me for imposing on you, Mrs. Roberts. But I know who you are. You're the wife of Lloyd Roberts who wrote this marvelous play for Miss Crane.

KAREN.   *(Dryly.)* My husband would agree with you. *He* thinks it's marvelous too.

EVE.   I've seen you come in or go out with Miss Crane so many times. Finally I asked one of the fans who you were and she told me. Could you do me a favor — a tremendous favor?

KAREN.   Not until I know what it is.

EVE.   I wondered if I could go inside — to the dressing room — and actually *meet* Miss Crane? There's no one waiting here tonight but me.

KAREN.   Absolutely out of the question. *(She starts to go into the theatre.)*

EVE.   *(Grabbing her.)* Please, Mrs. Roberts. Please! If I could only meet Margo Crane in person — just to shake her hand — it would be the thrill of my lifetime.

KAREN.   But Margo hates you autograph hounds.

EVE.   I'm not an autograph hunter, Mrs. Roberts. That's for morons. I'm a real admirer of her art. I've seen the play over and over again. I want to tell her what profound pleasure she's given me. What inner joy! She's a magnificent artiste. Surely any superb actress likes to know that her work is appreciated? Even by a nobody like me.

KAREN.   Well, Margo has quite an ego. I'll give you that.

EYE.   Is it too much to ask? I've tried to speak to her when she's been leaving the theatre but she's always in such a rush.

KAREN.   Margo's very shy. She dislikes meeting strangers. It's much better for you to admire her across the footlights. Now, if you'll excuse me ... *(She moves away but Eve stops her again.)*

EYE.   Mrs. Roberts, I've paid to see this play — from a balcony seat — over fifty times. *(Karen's interest is arrested.)* Fifty-seven to be exact. Don't you think that deserves one little minute of Miss Crane's time?

KAREN.   *(After a pause.)* There might be a publicity angle.... Wait here. I don't have much influence but I'll see what I can do. It depends on what offstage role she's playing tonight. If it's Lady Bountiful, you might have a chance. But I can't promise anything. If I don't send someone for you in ten minutes, you'd better go home. It's a nasty night. *(She goes through the door, into the theatre. Eve leans against the wall. There is an almost feline smile of satisfaction on her face. The light fades out on Eve and comes up on Margo's dressing room. This room has two doors. One, in the R. wall, to the passage, and one in the U. wall, to a private lavatory. A dressing table and mirror are against the left wall. [NOTE: This wall may be imaginary or real at the discretion of the director.] There is a chaise lounge; a small screen hides the lavatory door. In front of the screen is a stool or small chair. Wherever any wall space is available there are hooks on which are hanging various dresses that Margo uses in the part she has just finished playing. Three people are seen in the dressing room. The woman is Margo Crane. She is a scintillating personality and wears her forty-five years as if they were thirty. Like most great actresses, she is not beautiful, but her looks are different, arresting and exciting. Her husband, Clement Howell, is sitting on the stool. He is about Margo's age [or a little older], sophisticated, wealthy and a strong personality in his own right. Lloyd Roberts is stretched out on the chaise lounge, smoking a cigarette and drinking a highball. He is a good-looking intellectual of about sixty. He wears glasses. Margo is dressed in an untidy wrapper and is making herself up for the street.)*

MARGO.   What I want to know is, how did the little bitch look from the front?

CLEMENT.   She has thick ankles, a scrawny neck and a face like a box.

MARGO.   *(Pleased.)* In other words she's perfect casting.

LLOYD.   *(Disgruntled.)* I knew we should have taken that Wilcox girl from Ashley Morris. She was much more attractive. I wrote nothing in the play to indicate that the actress should be an ugly duckling.

MARGO.   This girl has much more talent than Audrey. More ... sincerity.

CLEMENT.   *(Quietly.)* My dear intolerable wife — you chose this girl to replace Audrey for the simple reason that Audrey was much too good-looking.

MARGO.   Nonsense! The careless creature got pregnant. Am I to blame for an act of God?

CLEMENT.   Be honest for a change. You were delighted that she had to leave the cast. The one thing you can't abide is a pretty ingenue.

MARGO.   That's not quite fair. I could hold my own on the stage with any young girl who ever lived. I am never jealous.

CLEMENT.   No. But you're always cautious. Particularly in this play, because you're playing a girl of twenty-five and you're forty-five.

MARGO.   I'm thirty-five.

CLEMENT.   That was ten years ago. Lloyd knows your age. Why put on this kitten act in front of him?

LLOYD.   Margo, you can be any age you want to be — on the stage. For instance, there didn't seem to be any difference tonight between you and this new girl, as far as age went. You were perfectly convincing as contemporaries. But what made me furious was her bad timing. You lost two of your biggest yocks because of her. *(Karen knocks on the door and enters.)*

KAREN.   Hi, everybody!

LLOYD.   Hello, darling. Welcome to the lesser cat house of the Circle Theatre Zoo. We're scratching the new ingenue to bits. *(He moves his feet off the chaise lounge to allow Karen to sit.)* Sit here.

MARGO.   Hello, honey.

KAREN.   Hello. How did she do?

LLOYD.   She got through without drying up.

KAREN.   Is that all? I thought she looked good when I saw her rehearsing with the understudies.

LLOYD.   Seeing her with the understudies and seeing her with Margo is not a fair comparison. Margo has no understudy. So the girl had to rehearse her best scenes with the stage manager. It was pretty tough on her. One run-through with you, Margo, is not enough.

MARGO.   I have better things to do than rehearse my tail off with every replacement.

KAREN.   I agree with Margo. She shouldn't overwork. Incidentally, I thought it might be a good idea to put the girl in a pair of horn-rimmed glasses. It would give her more character.

MARGO.   Karen, I think that's brilliant.

CLEMENT.   Stop playing up to Margo, Karen. Do you want to destroy this kid completely? The only thing she's got is a pair of eyes.

KAREN.   Oh — speaking of kids, there's one outside in the rain. I promised her I'd bring her in to meet you, Margo.

MARGO.   *(Outraged.)* You did *what*, Karen? You know how I feel about those stage door drips!

KAREN.   This one's a little different. She's not just a hysterical fan. She doesn't even want an autograph. She's a *real* admirer. She's sincere. She wants to pay homage. She hangs around the stage alley like a little wet cat.

CLEMENT.   Does she wear a shabby red coat?

KAREN.   That's the one.

MARGO.   I've seen that character. She huddles against the wall and peers at me as if I were a Martian or something.

KAREN.   Because, to her, you're a superwoman from an-

11

other planet. Please see her, Margo. I wouldn't bore you if I didn't think she deserved it.

MARGO. Why does she deserve it?

KAREN. For one thing, she's actually paid to see this play over fifty times.

MARGO. *(Impressed and pleased.)* Fifty times! Well, to coin a phrase, one can't have too much of a good thing.

KAREN. She thinks you're better than a good thing, my pet. To her, you're the only genius acting today. She's rabid on the subject.

MARGO. *(Almost purring.)* Intelligent as well as rabid!

CLEMENT. Get off that pedestal, Margo. Your ego is showing. *(There is a respectful knock on the door.)*

MARGO. Come in. I'm decent — *(Sharply, to her husband.)* Even if my vanity is exposed. *(Harvey enters. He is a nondescript, sycophantic stage manager, of undetermined age.)*

HARVEY. Pardon me, Miss Crane. *(To Clement.)* Mr. Howell, Miss Caswell wants to know if you want to rehearse her tomorrow. She's waiting to go home.

CLEMENT. Tell her not tomorrow. There's a matinee anyway. After two more performances I'll know better what scenes to work on.

HARVEY. Yes, Mr. Howell. *(He starts to go.)*

CLEMENT. Tell her she did well. We're very pleased.

HARVEY. Sir, we lost quite a few laughs.

CLEMENT and LLOYD. *(Together.)* We know that!...

HARVEY. *(A little unnerved.)* Of course, sir. I was certain you'd both noticed it.

MARGO. Harvey, stop dithering! Pop out to the stage door and tell a fan in a red coat who's hanging around that she can come in for exactly two seconds.

HARVEY. *(Staggered.)* What, Miss Crane? I thought —

MARGO. Then stop thinking. Mrs. Roberts has at last prevailed on me to interview a member of my adoring public.

HARVEY. Very well, Miss Crane. I'll send her in. *(He scampers out.)*

KAREN. Margo, you're an angel.

MARGO. I suddenly thought there might be some publicity angle here. If this half-wit has paid fifty times to sit at my feet, there may be a story for our unimaginative press agent.

KAREN. *(Wide-eyed.)* Why, Margo, that's brilliant of you. A publicity angle never occurred to me.

MARGO. *(Suddenly catching sight of herself in the mirror.)* My God, I'm a wreck! Hand me a drink, Clement, darling. I really need it. *(He does so. She continues to study her face.)* Lloyd, this is positively the last time I shall play a woman under thirty. I am not a female Dorian Grey.

LLOYD. Ellen Terry played Portia when she was sixty.

MARGO. I'll bet her Nerissa was a hundred. *(There is a timid knock on the door again.)* Come. *(Harvey opens the door and shows in a very nervous Eve.)* I presume this is the young person, Miss Crane. *(He withdraws quietly, closing the dressing room door. Eve stands quite still and stares at Margo. In fact, during the scene she seldom takes her eyes off her. There is a rather awkward pause before Karen comes to the rescue.)*

KAREN. Well, here you are, my dear. You have your greatest wish. Miss Crane has graciously consented to see you.

EVE. I'm overwhelmed, Miss Crane. This is the most exciting moment I've ever known.

MARGO. *(Flattered.)* Oh, surely not! I'm just a piece of Broadway furniture, that's all.

CLEMENT. Contemporary, not antique.

MARGO. *(Out of the corner of her mouth.)* Shut up.

EVE. You're much more than that, Miss Crane. You're one of the finest actresses in the world.

MARGO. *(Over-modest.)* You're much too young to know what you're talking about. What's your name, my dear?

EVE. Eve. Eve Harrington.

MARGO. This cynical old poop here is my husband and producer, Mr. Howell.

EVE. How do you do, Sir.

CLEMENT. Good evening.

MARGO. And this sour-faced owl is Mrs. Roberts' husband. He wrote our play.

LLOYD. *(With humor.)* Our *very good* play! *(He rises and shakes her hand.)*

EVE. I congratulate you, Mr. Roberts. No one can write for Miss Crane the way you can.

CLEMENT. Don't tell him that. He'll want a higher royalty.

LLOYD. Have you seen any other of my plays besides this one, Miss Harrington?

EVE. I first saw Miss Crane in Chicago. *(To Margo.)* It was when you were on tour last season in Mr. Roberts' last play, *The Second Hand Wife.* I can't tell you, Miss Crane, what seeing you on the stage did for me. You completely altered the whole course of my life.

MARGO. I did? For God's sake, how?

EVE. I couldn't get your performance out of my mind. It haunted me night and day. It was almost like a religious experience — like being converted. From that moment on my life suddenly had direction. I knew that I had to come to New York where there was good theatre all the time. And where Margo Crane played almost every season in a new play. I particularly wanted to see you with an original cast, not with a lot of replacements. Forgive me for saying so, but your supporting company in Chicago was very inadequate.

MARGO. I agree with you, Eve. I had a real pack of dogs on that tour. You see, Clement, dear? The public aren't fooled. They *do* know good acting when they see it.

CLEMENT. Very well, my love. Next time you take half your salary and I'll give you a better cast.

MARGO. Don't let's discuss sordid things like money in front of this idealistic child.... *(To Eve.)* Now that you've seen me with worthier actors, what is your impression?

EVE. It helps. A great work of art is always set off better by the right frame.

MARGO. *(A little pompously.)* How true!... I understand you've seen our play several times.

EVE. I come every Tuesday night, like tonight. And always to the Saturday matinee. It's cheaper, you know. And then I never fail to come one other night, depending on when I can get a seat. A balcony seat, of course. Sometimes I stand. I don't mind standing because I sit most of the day.

MARGO. I presume you're working while you're sitting?

EVE.   Yes, Miss Crane. I'm a stenographer — in a law office on Wall Street. But I hate it. My days are just a matter of existing until I can go to the theatre again to see you.

KAREN.   There now, Margo! Don't you think Miss Harrington deserved to meet you?

MARGO.   *(Now the modest great lady.)* She makes me very humble. I never feel I deserve it when people praise me. *(Clement almost chokes.)*

EVE.   *(Rapturously.)* You bring great joy, Miss Crane. You take people out of their humdrum existence and give them beauty, art and escape. If it weren't for artists like yourself, little people like me would have no color or excitement in their lives. When I'm watching you I'm in another world — a glamorous, magical world.

MARGO.   That's quite a speech, isn't it, boys? *(To Eve.)* You have no idea what the theatre is really like, my girl. Glamour and fame are only a small part of it. The road is long and hard and when you get to the top it's a constant battle to stay up there.

EVE.   I suppose it must be. I wish I knew more about it. I could sit at your feet and listen to you talk about your art for hours.

MARGO.   *(On an impulse.)* Now that gives me an idea. *(She turns to Karen.)* Why don't we take Miss Harrington back to your apartment for some supper, Karen?

EVE.   *(Breathlessly.)* Oh, Miss Crane, I wouldn't want to intrude.

MARGO.   I insist. I so seldom have the opportunity to meet the youth of today; an actress of my age ought to be around young people. It helps to keep one ageless. Oh, I see plenty of young *actresses,* but they don't count. They're obsessed with themselves. They only have one thing in their heads: their careers. They flatter me to get something out of me. But you're different, Eve. You're sincere. I can sense that.

EVE.   I can't imagine anything I'd rather do, Miss Crane, than spend an evening with you. But if you're going to Mrs. Roberts' house, perhaps she'd rather I didn't come.

KAREN.   If Margo would like you to join us, Eve, you're

most welcome.

EVE. That's terribly nice of you, Mrs. Roberts. I can't tell you how grateful I am. *(There is a knock on the door. A maid opens it and comes in.)*

MARGO. Oh, Leila, did you cope with that grease spot?

LEILA. It's out. *(She crosses over to a peg which is behind Eve.)* Pardon me. *(Eve steps aside.)*

MARGO. Leila, this is Miss Eve Harrington. She's one of my admirers.

LEILA. Then what's she doing in here?

MARGO. I invited her. Sometimes I like to meet my fans face to face.

LEILA. Since when? Usually you say they're a bunch of —

MARGO. *(Snapping.)* That will do!... *(She turns to the others with a sweet smile.)* Now, all of you, please clear out. Leila has to help me into my clothes. Take Eve out to the car, Karen. I'll be with you in less than five minutes.

KAREN. *(Getting up.)* Come on, Eve. You'll have to sit up front with the chauffeur. *(Karen goes.)*

EVE. I'll ride curled up in the trunk if I have to.

LLOYD. *(Leading her out of the door.)* We're not kidnapping you. *(Clement hesitates in the doorway and turns to his wife.)*

CLEMENT. Pussycat, I think you're crazy sometimes. We know nothing about this girl. She might be a kleptomaniac and walk off with one of Karen's silver ashtrays.

MARGO. You always try to pull down anyone who builds me up. It won't hurt me to give this child a happy evening.

CLEMENT. Such generosity doesn't suit you, darling. You're not the type. It's out of character.

MARGO. You're out of character too. Or blind. If that girl was properly dressed she'd be quite an eyeful. Didn't you notice that 22 waist and 36 bust?

CLEMENT. I must be slipping. Thanks for the tip. I'll take a second look. *(He goes good-naturedly as Margo throws off her robe and steps into the dress Leila holds out for her. The lights dim. A few seconds later the lights come up, revealing Karen's library. This is a cozy room, lined with books. There is a small portable television set on a moveable trolley by a wall. There is a comfortable leather couch in the center of the room, a low table in front of it, and two easy chairs sit on either side of it. They've been eating buffet style, but are now drinking after-dinner coffee. Eve is sitting on a cushion beside the cocktail table. Clement is in the chair on Margo's right and Lloyd is in the left chair. The men are eating off tiny little "nest" tables. Margo is in the middle of talking about herself.)*

MARGO.   So you see, my dear, you've got to be shot with a streak of luck, if you're going to be successful on the stage. For instance, if I hadn't got into that subway train that morning — if I'd missed it by a few seconds — I'd never have run into Gilbert's stage manager, who tipped me off that he was looking for an ingenue.

EVE.   *(Intensely.)* But you *did* get the part. That means you were good. You had the talent in the first place.

CLEMENT.   Exactly. Lucky breaks are no use if you haven't the ability to take advantage of them.

LLOYD.   Luck and talent go together like ham and eggs.

EVE.   I don't want to presume, Miss Crane, but I can't help feeling Mr. Howell has done his part in making your career such a success.

CLEMENT.   Thank you, Eve. I need a champion in my corner sometimes.

EVE.   I've read lots of biographies of actresses and it seems to me that all the ones who've reached the top have had a brilliant man in the background. Someone who has helped them choose their plays, or has directed them; or a fine playwright who has written for them.

CLEMENT.   You're right, Eve. I do all the things you say, except write for Margo. I leave that to Lloyd here. *(Very proudly.)* Between us we've made her the greatest box office attraction in New York.

MARGO.   You make me sound as if I've had nothing to do with it. As if I've just been the harp and you've plucked the strings.

CLEMENT.   I don't think harp is quite the right instrument. It would be more appropriate to call you a bongo drum. I'm the witch doctor who beats the devil out of you.

MARGO.   Don't listen to him, Eve. He's like all producers and directors. He thinks he's Svengali.... However, I think I've talked quite enough about myself. You've hardly said a word. I want to hear about you. Where do you come from originally, darling? Begin at the beginning.

EVE.   I'm afraid it's a pretty dreary story. I'm from Milwaukee. My parents were Swedish. They didn't have much money. I'm one of six children. Somehow I managed to finish high school. I wanted to go to the University of Wisconsin and study drama but there was no money to send me to college. Then one day in the summer Mother and Daddy went out on Lake Michigan in a boat. A squall came up, the boat overturned somehow and they were both drowned ... *(She pauses for a moment, then goes quietly on.)* So I got a job in a restaurant waiting on tables. That's where I met the boy I married. Harrington is my married name. My real name is Swanson. Ricky had volunteered for the Air Force, but we had a week's honeymoon before he went away. We spent it in Chicago. He was the one who took me to see Miss Crane on the stage there. After he went off to Texas to start his basic training I returned to the restaurant and went on working. The manager was a horrible man. A real lecher. When he found out I'd got married and that my husband was away he became — impossible. Finally I couldn't take it any more. I'd saved up a little money, so I went back to Chicago. I was hoping you might return there, Miss Crane, in another play.... Well, I got a job in a restaurant in the Loop and began to go to night school to study shorthand and typing. After six months at the business school, I secured my first job — in an office. By this time Ricky was through with his training and had become a pilot. I'd just had a letter from him saying he'd found a place for us to live and that he wanted me to join him in Texas. I was getting ready to leave Chicago when I got the telegram. *(She pauses, unable to continue for a moment.)*

MARGO.   *(Softly.)* The telegram?

EVE.   There'd been an accident — a training accident. The whole crew was killed.

MARGO.   *(Moved.)* What a sad story! First your parents.

Then your husband. And you're so young.

EVE. *(Without self-pity.)* Suddenly I felt I had nothing to live for. And then I remembered you, Miss Crane.

MARGO. At a time like that you remembered *me?*

EVE. Yes. I remembered how thrilled I'd been with your performance. How you'd sort of taken me out of myself. That might happen again, I thought to myself. If anyone can make me forget my troubles, it's Margo Crane. Maybe she can help me to go on living even without Ricky. So instead of going to Texas I came to New York. I found a job and a place to live. And I found something to do with my evenings that makes them bearable. Because of the theatre, Miss Crane, and because of you — well, I've learned to live with my sorrow. *(There is a pause. Margo is practically in tears.)*

MARGO. I think that's the most touching story I've ever heard. I never dreamed that I would inspire someone to go on living.

EVE. That's exactly what you did, Miss Crane. I have a lot of boring letters to write — business letters. I'm more of a secretary than a stenographer. Frankly, I think my boss imposes on me but since he keeps me so busy I don't complain.

KAREN. In what way does he impose on you?

EVE. Well, he leaves a lot to my discretion. I answer most of his letters now. Then I make appointments for him or refuse them. I know by this time the people he wants to see and those he wants to avoid. It's quite a responsibility.

MARGO. *(Suddenly.)* Eve — how would you like to work for me?

EVE. *(Opening her eyes very wide.)* In — in what way, Miss Crane?

MARGO. As a sort of private secretary. Part business, part social.

CLEMENT. Now wait a minute, Pussycat —

MARGO. You shut up. You know I need a secretary. You're the one who's always complaining that I never answer letters, or take care of my checkbook properly or return scripts. I'm always forgetting appointments. Eve could make herself useful to me in all sorts of ways ...

EVE.   I write a very good letter, Miss Crane. I have a fabulous memory. And I won a prize for spelling.

MARGO.   Of course, your hours will be more erratic, but at least you won't have to pay to go to the theatre. You can watch me from the wings as often as you want to.

EVE.   It would be heaven.

MARGO.   Then it's settled. Write down the address for her, Clement.

CLEMENT.   *(Taking a notebook from his pocket, tearing off a page, and writing.)* You're sure you're not railroading Miss Harrington into something, Margo? She might like to think it over.

MARGO.   What's there to think over about going to heaven? Write down our address, Clement. *(He does so and hands it to Eve.)*

EVE.   I'll be there at nine o'clock in the morning, Sir. If you don't mind, Mrs. Roberts, I'll be running along. I'd like to be fresh for tomorrow.

LLOYD.   I'll take Eve home.

EVE.   Please don't bother, Mr. Roberts. I can get the subway straight down to the village.

LLOYD.   At this hour of the night? I won't allow it. I'll put you in a taxi ...

EVE.   Good night, Mrs. Roberts. Thank you ever so much. I hope I'll be able to repay you some day.

KAREN.   Good night, Eve. I guess we'll be seeing a lot more of each other.

EVE.   It's a dream. I simply haven't taken it in yet. Good night, Mr. Howell, I'll make sure Miss Crane doesn't regret her generosity. Good night, Miss Crane. *(Very simply.)* Thank you. *(Even and Lloyd go out.)*

KAREN.   Margo, you're completely unpredictable. I asked you to see this girl for two minutes and in two hours she's one of the family.

MARGO.   That's typically me. I never do things by halves.

CLEMENT.   And you never do things with any thought either. You're so God-damned emotional you let yourself be

20

carried away.

KAREN. *(Anxious to escape a scene.)* Well, while you let Margo win another fight, Clement, I'll go find a bottle of brandy. *(Karen picks up a couple of coffee cups and goes out.)*

CLEMENT. *(Quietly.)* I don't mean to carp, darling, but I really don't quite approve of this business.

MARGO. That girl's loyalty personified. I feel it in my bones.

CLEMENT. You and your bones! You didn't even ask the girl for a reference.

MARGO. A woman's intuition is enough. I'm never wrong about people.

CLEMENT. What about that chauffeur you hired who stole the car?

MARGO. He was a man. But I am never wrong about my own sex. The worst that can happen is that she'll turn out to be inefficient, in which case I'll fire her.

CLEMENT. Oh, I'm sure she'll be efficient. That isn't quite what I meant.

MARGO. Well, what *do* you mean?

CLEMENT. It's just a feeling. I can't quite pin it down.

MARGO. It's probably her name. Men have been suspicious of girls called Eve since the first one listened to a snake.

CLEMENT. All right, Margo. I see it's useless to argue with you. I'll put her on the payroll tomorrow.... On second thought I think what I'm really worried about is not what the poor child will do to you, it's what you might do to her. You might fire her as impulsively as you engaged her. That girl's in seventh heaven. Kicking her out of it might have serious consequences. We don't want a suicide on our hands. That would hardly be good publicity.

MARGO. *(Suddenly down to earth and reasonable.)* Yes, you're right! I see that. You always are, when it comes to practical things that affect my career. I suppose I was a bit over-impulsive but when I feel generous I have to *be* generous. If the girl doesn't turn out well, I promise I won't do anything rash. I'll let you handle it.

CLEMENT. Good girl. Now you're making sense. *(Satisfied*

with his victory, Clement lights a cigar as the lights dim out. Once more the spotlight appears D.C. and Karen steps into it. She is differently dressed and wears a fur coat this time.)

KAREN.   ... I didn't discover how things were working out for them for nearly a month, because Lloyd and I left for Florida a couple of days after that supper. He was supposed to be finishing a new play for Margo and was under the delusion that the sunshine would inspire him. He was having the usual second act trouble, and all the sun did was give him an excuse *not* to write. So finally, just before Christmas, I managed to uproot him and get him back to his typewriter in New York ... I'd forgotten all about Eve and it gave me quite a shock when I dropped in to see Margo during a matinee and Eve opened the dressing room door. *(The lights black out on Karen, who disappears into the darkness. They come up again, revealing Margo's dressing room. It has changed quite a lot. It has been fixed with curtains, the chairs and chaise lounge have been reupholstered. Margo's dressing room table is as neat as a Swede can make it. A tray with silver-looking covered dishes sits on a little table near the chaise. Eve is seated in front of the mirror making herself up — trying out Margo's eye-shadow. She, too, looks different. She is dressed in a neat little suit and she has obviously been to a good hairdresser. After a moment she goes over to Margo's dresses that are hanging against the wall, takes one down and holds it against herself. She is turning this way and that in front of the mirror admiring the effect when there is a knock at the door. She hangs up the dress quickly, pats her lipstick to tone it down, then goes and opens the door.)*

EVE.   Why, Mrs. Roberts! *(Karen comes in.)*

KAREN.   Eve! I hardly recognize you.

EVE.   How wonderful to see you again! What a lovely Florida tan you have!

KAREN.   How do you know I've been to Florida?

EVE.   I've seen the postcards you've sent Miss Crane. I answer all her mail now.

KAREN.   Oh, of course. How's everything working out?

EVE.   I've never been so happy. Miss Crane's been an absolute angel to me. When I remember what my life was like

B.C. — before Crane, I mean — I can't think how I managed to exist. Now, every moment is so stimulating. I meet all sorts of celebrities; I talk to famous people on the phone; I reply to their letters. But, best of all, I come to the theatre every performance now. I double as secretary and dresser.

KAREN. *(Very surprised.)* What happened to Leila?

EVE. Miss Crane put her back in the penthouse kitchen.

KAREN. That's fantastic! She's been Margo's dresser for ten years.

EVE. She was very good at looking after the costumes and all that but, as I pointed out to Miss Crane, she was terribly untidy. This dressing room used to be a mess.

KAREN. How did Leila like being demoted to the kitchen?

EVE. Not too well, I'm afraid. I try to spare Miss Crane any kind of incompetence so that she can concentrate on her work.

KAREN. How's the play going?

EVE. Better than ever. As usual, the matinee is sold out. *(She picks up a little clock on the dressing table and looks at it.)* The curtain will come down in about five minutes. I wonder — could I ask you to do something for me, Mrs. Roberts?

KAREN. What do you want, Eve?

EVE. *(Awkwardly.)* I — I don't quite know how to put it. I'm afraid you may think what I have in mind is wrong.

KAREN. You want to leave Margo. Is that it?

EVE. Anything but. I want to *understudy* her. *(Karen looks at her, very puzzled.)*

KAREN. I don't understand, Eve. You're not an actress.

EVE. Not a *professional* one, no. But I did a lot of amateur acting in high school. The night I went to your house I told all of you how I'd wanted to go to Wisconsin to study drama. Don't you remember?

KAREN. Yes, I recall you said something of the kind. But you didn't suggest you had any serious ambition to go on the stage.

EVE. I didn't have any — not that night. But now that I've been exposed to the atmosphere of a real theatre, I've caught the fever again. I want to be part of it, as an actress.

Of course, I'd go on working for Miss Crane as usual. But I have a lot of time on my hands — particularly in the morning. That's when Harvey rehearses the understudies.

KAREN. But, Eve, you'd never get a chance to *play* the part. Nobody ever goes on for Margo.

EVE. I'm well aware of that. Just the same I'd have the experience of working with professional actors. *(Karen paces the room, thoughtfully. She doesn't seem too anxious to go along with Eve's idea.)*

KAREN. Have you talked this matter over with Margo? Does she know you want to be an actress?

EVE. Oh, I wouldn't dare tell her. I know how she feels about young actresses. She might turn against me.

KAREN. Yes, she very well might. In Margo's vocabulary "ingenue" is a dirty word.

EVE. That's why it would take someone with great tact, like yourself, Mrs. Roberts, to suggest that I be her understudy. Actually, I would be a help, you know. The understudies are always complaining that they have to rehearse with a stage manager mumbling Margo's part. I know the part already. I've taken it down in shorthand from the wings. I know every word, every gesture, every position.

KAREN. You certainly haven't let any grass grow under your feet.

EVE. Anyone would be foolish not to take advantage of an opportunity like mine.

KAREN. Yes, I'll have to agree with you there.

EVE. Perhaps if you could stress to Miss Crane that it might help me to make a little extra money, she might agree to the idea. You wouldn't have to bring the matter up that I have any serious hopes of becoming a professional actress.

KAREN. The truth is, Eve, I've always thought it a mistake not to have Margo's part covered. But for a star of her caliber, they always engage a very experienced standby.

EVE. Miss Crane is too big a star ever to be replaced by anyone. I'd just work at rehearsals. Not that I'm not good casting for the part, as far as age goes. Elizabeth is only supposed to be twenty-five. If I did have the opportunity, you could come in some day and watch a rehearsal. I promise you that if you think I have no talent, I'll take your word for it and forget all my dreams. At best, you'd have a chance to see what I can do.

KAREN. *(Now won over.)* Well, Eve, I can't see any great harm in it. I can't promise anything, but I can try.

EVE. Then it's as good as settled. *(There is a faint sound of applause off R.)* Listen! There's the curtain! She'll be in in a minute.... Incidentally, did you drop by for any particular reason? You haven't said.

KAREN. My husband is busy this evening. I thought Margo might come out to Sardi's with me for dinner.

EVE. *(Pointing to the tray.)* She's had it sent in. But if you could persuade her to go out with you, that might be just the right moment to bring up what we've been talking about.

KAREN. We'll see what sort of mood she's in. *(Karen opens the dressing room door. The applause is louder.)* The old ladies are knocking themselves out. Listen to that.

EVE. Isn't it marvelous, Mrs. Roberts! Sometimes when I'm standing in the wings listening to them, it gives me a lump in my throat. That's when I start to imagine how marvelous it would be if *I* were adored like that. To have all that power over an audience. What a thrill! To be a great actress like Miss Crane must be the most marvelous life in the world.

MARGO. *(Off-stage. Yelling.)* Harvey, find out which idiot turned up the heat. I warn you, if it happens tonight, I'll play the last act stark naked. *(She comes into the room and sees Karen.)* My God, if it isn't that Florida beachcomber! *(She kisses Karen affectionately.)* I hate you, you bitch. You look much too healthy. Here we've been slaving away, earning royalties for you and your cantankerous husband, and you sit in the sun and wallow. *(She unzips her sequined stage dress and steps out of it. It lies on the floor until Eve picks it up and hangs it up. Margo now wears a slip.)*

KAREN. *(Laughing.)* Why pretend to be envious? You hate the sun. It gives you wrinkles.

MARGO. *(To Eve.)* She's a spiteful woman. She always tells me the truth ...

KAREN. Put on a dress. You're coming with me to Sardi's for dinner.

MARGO. *(Pointing to the tray.)* Sorry. Sardi's is here.

EVE. I'll eat it for you, Miss Crane. Then I won't have to go out. *(She gets Margo's street shoes and helps her into them.)* Why don't you accept Mrs. Roberts' invitation? It always gives everyone in Sardi's such a thrill to see you.

MARGO. What the hell! I might as well be gracious once in a while. But I'm damned if I'll take off all my makeup. I'll just pat it down.

EVE. *(Holding out a street dress.)* Step into this. You won't disturb your hair. *(Margo does so. Eve zips up the back.)*

MARGO. Do you know what Eve did that was absolutely marvelous? She got a plumber in here and got the johnny fixed. It's stopped sounding like Niagara Falls. Now it's an absolute pleasure to pull the chain.

EVE. *(Modestly.)* Miss Crane, you embarrass me.

MARGO. *(Patting down her makeup.)* I know I'm a damned fool to praise you so much. You're ridiculously underpaid.

EVE. *(Flashing a look at Karen.)* I'm perfectly content with what you give me, Miss Crane.

KAREN. Margo, I have an idea about how we could slip Eve a few extra bucks.

MARGO. If you're thinking of bribing her away from me for Lloyd, I'll consider it a stab in the back — like stealing my cook.

KAREN. Speaking of cooks, Eve tells me Leila is back in the kitchen.

MARGO. Yes. And she's taking her revenge on me by cooking everything in butter.... Well, I guess I'm ready. *(Eve holds out Margo's mink coat which she slips on.)* I wish I could have a good drink. Maybe I'll risk a small double martini. We have a theatre party tonight so if I fluff a line or two it won't matter. They'll all be half crocked too. *(Karen and Margo leave. Left alone, Eve hangs up Margo's stage dress properly. She then proceeds to put the dressing table in order which Margo, in one minute, had put into disarray. She goes over to Margo's tray and peeks under the covered dishes that are sitting on hot plates. As she*

26

does this, there is a knock at the door.)

EVE.   Come ... *(Harvey, the stage manager, enters. Now that he is in the presence of someone who is an employee like himself, he is no longer so oily.)*

HARVEY.   Hi, Sexpot!

EVE.   Hello, Don Juan!

HARVEY.   I saw the First Lady of the Theatre leave with her Pet Cat. Where have they gone?

EVE.   Out to dinner.

HARVEY.   Good! That means you're on your own for a couple of hours. *(He comes over to her, puts a proprietary arm around her waist and kisses her on the mouth, obviously not for the first time. Eve pushes him away gently.)*

EVE.   Please, Harvey! Not in here. She might come back. She's always forgetting something.

HARVEY.   *(Reluctant to let her go.)* I'm going out for a bite of food myself. I'll be back in half an hour. Will you come upstairs to my room for a little while?

EVE.   My God, you're insatiable!

HARVEY.   I'm mad about you, Eve. Please come up to my room.

EVE.   All right, I'll see — if she doesn't come back early.... Darling, I did what you suggested. I persuaded Mrs. Roberts to ask her. I think it may be okay.

HARVEY.   I'm sure it's a better idea than *my* mentioning it.

EVE.   You've got to support the suggestion. Tell them it's an excellent idea — that you've always felt you can't direct the understudies properly when you have to be up on the stage half the time reading the old girl's part.

HARVEY.   I already told you I'll back up the idea. I want to help you get ahead. Honestly I do.

EVE.   So long as we understand each other, Angel. *(This time she kisses him. The kiss is anything but platonic.)* Now run along and let me eat my dinner.

HARVEY.   I'll hurry back.

EVE.   And, Harvey — remember, if this gets out — if they ever suspect there's anything between us — I'll see that you ...

HARVEY. *(Interrupting.)* Why should I open my mouth? I'm a married man. *(He winks at her and goes, shutting the door behind him. Eve takes the lid off the chicken pot pie and prepares to serve herself a portion on a plate. She also pours herself out some coffee. There is a knock on the door and Mr. Howell comes in without announcing himself.)*

CLEMENT. Good evening, Eve. I just met Harvey at the stage door. He said my wife had left the theatre. Where did she go?

EVE. *(Rising.)* Sardi's, Mr. Howell. Mrs. Roberts dropped in unexpectedly.

CLEMENT. Oh! Well, I'll go over and join them. *(He starts to go. Eve stops him.)*

EVE. Mr. Howell, can you spare a second? I'd like to talk to you about something.

CLEMENT. What is it, Eve?

EVE. It's something Mrs. Roberts suggested to me. We had a few moments alone together just now. She said that when she and Mr. Roberts were in Florida, he was worried because Miss Crane has no understudy. Apparently it's been on his mind ever since Miss Caswell had to rehearse with Harvey. Harvey's such a terrible actor. Mr. Roberts thinks it's a great handicap to the understudies, as well as any other replacements that might have to come in. Mrs. Roberts thought it might be a good idea if I covered Miss Crane's part.

CLEMENT. You, Eve? Do you think you're capable of doing that?

EVE. I know I'd never be allowed to go on. But I have done a bit of acting. I know all the lines. It would simply be a convenience to the other actors.

CLEMENT. But you're not a professional. You'd have to join Actors Equity.

EVE. I wouldn't mind doing that. Anyway, it's up to you, Mr. Howell. There's one other point that occurred to me too. When we go on tour, I can take over Miss Caswell's understudy as well. I'll be going anyway. This means you would save an extra salary.

CLEMENT. *(Dryly.)* For the first time this idea begins to

appeal to me!... Very well, Eve. If that's what Lloyd wants, it's all right with me.

EVE. *(With a gush of enthusiasm.)* Oh, Mr. Howell, thank you! Thank you very much. The extra salary will be a godsend. I have to dress so much better now. My expenses have gone up with hairdressers and everything. You really are a most generous person. I'd do anything to show you how grateful I am. *(She throws her arms around his neck and kisses him on the lips. At first this might be interpreted as girlish enthusiasm, but as she continues to cling to him, we see that this is not just a "thank you" kiss but an offer. Clement's first instinct is to respond, but he restrains himself and gently pushes her away.)*

CLEMENT. Thank you, Eve. That was quite a reward from a weeping widow. I enjoyed it. If I didn't know you were so loyal to my wife, I might misconstrue your enthusiasm. *(He gives her a long look.)* May I give you a bit of advice, Eve — should you ever take up acting seriously?

EVE. *(Thin-lipped.)* What is it?

CLEMENT. Never overplay your part. *(He turns abruptly and leaves without a further word. Eve, furious at being rejected, stamps her foot in anger. After a moment or two she simmers down, then resumes her seat at the little table and begins to eat her meal thoughtfully. The lights dim out. When they come up again, the D. area is illuminated by a shaded work light. Harvey is rehearsing Eve to get her up in the part. He is reading from the script. She is working from memory.)*

HARVEY. *(Reading flatly and badly.)* "If you've anything on your mind, say it. I despise — insinuations."

EVE. *(Acting amazingly well.)* "I despise hypocrisy. You've got a date tomorrow night with that dancer, Jayne Case."

HARVEY. *(Sharply.)* "What do you know of Miss Case?"

EVE. "That she's your mistress!"

HARVEY. ... "Has it occurred to you that your accusation may be incorrect? I do happen to be acquainted with a girl named Jayne Case — but only acquainted. She was in that musical I backed. I sometimes have dinner with her when I'm in town."

EVE. "Breakfast too. At Sutton Place. You pay the rent."

HARVEY. "Whoever told you that fairy story?"

EVE. "Without knowing it, Miss Case herself. It was a year ago. I saw a beautiful handbag in Dunhill's window. I didn't have much money with me but I knew you had a charge account there for your cigars, so I decided to go in and see if I could use it. When I went up to the counter a girl was buying an expensive photo frame. To my amazement I saw she was trying your photo in it for size. I couldn't help hearing what the girl said to the clerk. In fact, I deliberately listened. She said: 'Charge it to Mr. Russell Wain, 15 Wall Street, and send it to Miss Jayne Case, 1008 Sutton Place South, Penthouse E.' When the clerk commented on the distinguished appearance of the man in the photograph, Miss Case said: 'That's my fiancé. We're going to be married next year.' I walked out of the shop in a daze. I couldn't believe that you would be so double-faced. Unhappily I found out that there wasn't a shadow of a doubt."

HARVEY. *(After a pause.)* "Well, Elizabeth, I won't attempt to justify my actions. But there is one glaring error in your — investigations. You and your mother have always come first. Never, not for one second, have I contemplated breaking up my home and marrying Miss Case."

EVE. "I can't quite believe that, Daddy. You see, I've watched you lying regularly for over a year now."

HARVEY. "Then if everything I say is suspect, there doesn't seem to be anything more we can say to one another. You've closed your mind and hardened your heart against me."

EVE. *(Dramatically.)* "I'm sorry, Daddy. It's true. Nothing you can say will move me. Not ever again."

HARVEY. *(Claps hands.)* Curtain. Okay, Eve. That's it for this morning. It's time for lunch.

EVE. Oh dear. Can't we go on? I wanted to show Mr. Roberts what I could do with Act Two. *(Suddenly Lloyd and Karen appear in the auditorium and come down one of the aisles to the footlights. She wears her mink coat. You don't see her dress.)*

LLOYD. You don't have to show me, Eve. I've seen all I need to see.

EVE. *(Anxiously.)* You mean I'm terrible.

LLOYD. Quite the contrary. You're magnificent. Didn't I say that to you, Karen?

KAREN. He certainly did, Eve. I'm proud of you. You're excellent in the part. *(By now they have gone onto the stage by way of some steps leading up over the footlights.)*

HARVEY. I tell you this kid could keep the curtain up any time.

LLOYD. There's no doubt about it. In fact, Eve, you'd do a lot more than merely keep up the curtain. You'd give a first-rate performance. It's a revelation to me. You bring a whole new quality into the play. I don't understand it.

EVE. *(Sweetly.)* Perhaps it's because I'm the right age for the part — as you wrote it. Of course, I can't be compared to Miss Crane. She's in a class by herself. Way up there. But I do have youth.

LLOYD. What beats me is that my lines sound different somehow. They seem to have more rhythm.

EVE. It could be that I stick to the text as you wrote it, Mr. Roberts. Miss Crane does a lot of — revising. I asked her once why she changes the lines so much and she explained that she has to make them her own.

LLOYD. She sounds better when she uses mine. *(Eve turns to Karen.)*

EVE. Mrs. Roberts, I'm terribly grateful to you for dragging Mr. Roberts here. I know it must have been a bore for both of you. Harvey, thank you for all your help. *(To Lloyd.)* You know, Harvey is a wonderful director.

LLOYD. *(Unenthusiastically.)* Yes, he's very efficient!... Say, I've an idea. Why don't you let Karen and me take you out for a quick lunch? I'd like to give you a few pointers about the quarrel scene with the boy. It could be a little more unrestrained.

EVE. Oh, that would be marvelous! Can we go out the stage door? My coat's in Miss Crane's dressing room. *(She and Lloyd stroll R., towards the wings.)*

LLOYD. You see, this boy has no money and because you're so loaded he won't propose. Now you really have to turn on the waterworks in that scene. And you have to play on his inverted snobbery, so that — (*By now, they have disappeared into the wings. Karen has lingered behind for a moment.*)

KAREN.   Thank you, Harvey, for letting us come. I hope we weren't a nuisance.

HARVEY.   Not at all, Mrs. Roberts. I'm sorry I couldn't have the other understudies here. But they'd had their rehearsal this week and you know unions.

KAREN.   I do indeed. It's a wonder they allow us to work at all. I'm sorry we couldn' t come on the proper day.

HARVEY.   That's okay. The main thing was for you to see Eve. I wanted you to have confidence that she could go on. She's really great, isn't she?

KAREN.   Yes. We were both amazed. Thank you so much again. (*She leaves in the same direction as her husband and Eve. Harvey smiles with satisfaction. He leaves the stage in the opposite direction, the script tucked under his arm. The lights black out. When the lights go up again Eve is seated on the stool in front of the screen, sewing a button on one of Margo's dresses. Lloyd is lounging on the chaise lounge with his new script on his lap.*)

LLOYD.   You mean she hasn't given you a hint?

EVE.   Not a word, Mr. Roberts.

LLOYD.   But surely you must have an inkling? Even if you only overheard her talking to Clement.

EVE.   If they've discussed your script it must have been in the privacy of their bedroom — or when I haven't been around. I haven't gleaned the faintest idea as to whether Mr. Howell likes it or not. (*Pausing thoughtfully.*) It's very odd. I should have thought a new play by you, written especially for her, would have been their sole topic of conversation.

LLOYD.   I agree. It's rather worrying. Before, she's always let me know her reaction in a couple of days. I've been sitting up in Connecticut knocking myself out to finish it and now she keeps me waiting for a reaction.

EVE.   (*Wistfully.*) I wish *I* could read it. (*There is the sound of applause in the distance.*) That's the curtain. The matinee's over. (*She gets up and opens the dressing room door. The applause is now louder.*) Mr. Roberts, please don't think me forward, but I've been dying to ask you. Is there anything *I* could do in the play?

LLOYD. If there were I'd give it to you in a minute. But I was careful *not* to write a good ingenue part this time.

EVE. *(Sadly.)* I'm beginning to think I'll never get a break.

LLOYD. *(His mind elsewhere.)* Something will come along some day. Have patience. They aren't very enthusiastic this afternoon. They must be sitting on their hands. *(The applause dies away.)*

EVE. The house was only half full. I guess most people are away weekends during the summer. *(After hanging up the dress she was working on, she goes to the dressing table and starts putting out Margo's street makeup.)* Mr. Roberts — I wonder, could you recommend me to a couple of agents? I've met Mr. Hinkle, Miss Crane's agent, but he said he couldn't do anything for me because he hadn't seen me act.

LLOYD. Most of the bloodsuckers would say that. They don't recognize talent until it's dumped in their laps. *(Margo stalks into the dressing room like an avenging fury. She is dressed in the sequin evening gown we have seen once before.)*

MARGO. What an afternoon! I knock my brains out for a herd of commuting cows! And do they applaud? No! They sit on their cans and chew the cud! *(Focusing a beady eye on Lloyd.)* Aha! So Tennessee Bernard Shaw has arrived!

LLOYD. *(Rising.)* Hello, darling!

MARGO. Don't "darling" me. I'm livid with you. *(To Eve.)* Get me out of this shroud. And make it snappy. I've got a cocktail date at "21" with Bert Hinkle. *(During the following scene, Eve helps Margo out of her stage dress and into a dressing gown, after which Margo sits at the table, removes her stage makeup and puts on a street makeup and combs her hair. Eve effaces herself but listens to everything that is said with great concentration.)*

LLOYD. What do you mean, you've "got a date," Margo? I thought we were going to sit here and discuss my play.

MARGO. Then you've got another thought coming. I can say what I want to say in two sentences. I think the part stinks. I wouldn't play it if I were down to my last calorie.

LLOYD. *(Staggered.)* You're kidding!

MARGO. I was never more serious. How dare you write me

33

a character who's a twenty-five-year-old icicle?

LLOYD. Cora is twenty-six.

MARGO. That's a childish quibble! I think I'd better tell you the facts of life, Angel. Bert Hinkle is bringing Isaac Katz of International Pictures to meet me for cocktails. He's angling for me and I'm nibbling. They want me for a terrific role, a thirty-three-year-old, sexy divorcee, at a fabulous salary. I repeat — *sexy*. Hollywood is showing some sense for a change.

LLOYD. *(Thoroughly angry.)* So that's at the back of it. Plain, unadulterated greed! Hollywood money has turned you against playing in my play. It's not the part.

MARGO. Wrong again. It's only a three weeks' job in September. They finish with everyone quickly these days. When I come back I'll be perfectly free to do a Broadway play. But it won't be yours. It'll be by some other genius.

LLOYD. But what about the tour of this present play? Are you ditching that too?

MARGO. Clement can get Louise Anderson to do this crappy role. He's offered it to her and she's accepted ... *(Becoming a little more reasonable.)* Frankly, Lloyd, I'm tired to death of it. I'm bored. I've decided against it. I couldn't face a tour. I need a rest.

LLOYD. You've always said nothing bores you more than resting.

MARGO. It's no good arguing. I've made up my mind. I admit that if your new play had turned out the way I'd hoped, I would have done it after Christmas no matter how tired I felt. But the part is *not right for me.*

LLOYD. Can't we talk about it? I'd be willing to make some revisions.

MARGO. You can't change your whole basic situation. What possessed you to think I'd play a young girl who loses her husband to an older woman — and a Spanish woman at that?

LLOYD. What the hell has the woman's nationality got to do with it?

MARGO. *(Shouting.)* Nothing! But I don't lose my husband

to anybody of any nationality on any stage!... Also, this turgid muck isn't your *metier* at all. You've written a drama! A serious play. About a frigid girl. Do I look the frigid type, you blind booby? You must be out of your idiotic mind.

LLOYD. *(Heavily sarcastic.)* May I remind you, my pet, that my idiotic mind has written your last three hits?

MARGO.   Oh, shut up! Your vanity's gone to your typewriter.

LLOYD.   *My* vanity! That's rich! I suppose you think you've only got to step on a stage and read the bloody telephone book and the public will kiss your feet. I suppose you think you don't *need* a strong vehicle!

MARGO.   *(Snapping.)* I *do* need a vehicle. The right vehicle. Can't you get it into your head that I haven't the proper quality for Cora?

LLOYD.   No. Because actresses have no judgement. They're always winning Oscars for parts they're forced into playing.... Tell me this, does Clem agree this part's wrong for you?

MARGO.   Oh, he thinks you've written a play. He may even give you a production. But not with me in the lead. He's on my side about that.

LLOYD.   Who does he think *could* play the part?

MARGO.   He doesn't know. He says it's a tough role to cast. There aren't too many young stars who can emote. *(She has now finished her street makeup. She takes off her dressing gown and Eve helps her into her street dress.)*

LLOYD.   *(Trying flattery.)* That's the point, Margo. It's a part for a star — like you. It's got everything. Bitterness, compassion, pathos ...

MARGO.   *(Thumbing the table.)* And no *comedy*! Damn you! I'm a comedienne! Did you forget that this time? Or were you writing without me in mind? Were you so carried away with your creativeness that you forgot what shows me off to my best advantage? What infuriates me is that the script bears no resemblance to the original idea we talked over. It was agreed I was to play the older woman who lost her husband temporarily to the young girl and got him back in the end. Suddenly the whole thing's in reverse.

LLOYD. It didn't jell that way. The more I worked on the theme, the more it turned into a cliché. The moment I turned things around everything fell into place. The scenes wrote themselves.

MARGO. Well, they can *act* themselves without Margo Crane.

LLOYD. Margo, you're intolerable! What makes you think I can't have a hit if you're not in it?

MARGO. *(Sour-sweet.)* Well, let's face the facts, Honey Lamb. With me you've had three smashes. Before me, you had two Broadway flops, and one turkey that was roasted to death in Philadelphia.

LLOYD. I was learning my trade. You happened to come into my life after I'd learnt it.

MARGO. Nuts! When I optioned *Winter Foolishness* you had promise, nothing more. I've taught you everything you know. It was the changes *I* wanted, the cuts *I* wanted, the touches of character *I* insisted on, the bits of business *I* invented, plus Clement's direction, that saved your plays from mediocrity.

LLOYD. *(Outraged.)* So I'm nothing but a hack who strings a few sentences together for the great Margo Crane to transform into a play! That's funny, from an actress who can't even say the lines the way I write them.

MARGO. I don't say them the way you write them because half the time they don't "talk."

LLOYD. Poppycock! Psychotic poppycock! They talk all right. They talk in summer stock. They talk in amateur productions. They talk in movies. They talk when an understudy talks them at rehearsal. They talk an audience into laughter when second-rate actresses talk them in theatres all over the country. But you, the great *I Am*, you have to "make them your own." Well, write your own. See if I care, you conceited, spoilt, aging — soubrette! *(There is quite a long pause. Margo is stunned into silence at last. Suddenly all her anger seems to evaporate and she is polite and courteous — a little too polite.)*

MARGO. I think you'd better go, Lloyd. And please tell that sweet wife of yours, for whom I feel great sympathy, that in the circumstances, I must beg off coming to the country this weekend. I might castrate you before the Sunday was over. *(She crosses to the door and flings it open with a theatrical gesture.)* Good night, Mr. Ibsen. I regret I'm too old to play in your *Doll's House. (She sweeps out, leaving the door open.)*

EVE.   *(Calling — after a moment's silence.)* Miss Crane, you forgot your stole. Remember what air-conditioning does to your throat. *(She grabs a white woolly stole from a hanger and chases out after Margo.)*

LLOYD.   *(Shouting down the passage.)* Tie it around her neck and strangle her. *(He turns back into the room in a blind fury, picks up his script from the chaise lounge and flings it against the screen. It falls onto the floor in a mess amongst a row of shoes.)* Bitch! Bitch! Bitch! *(He storms out of the dressing room and down the hall. For a moment, the stage is empty. Then, after a pause, Eve returns. She closes the door and leans against it. The preceding scene seems to have given her a certain measure of satisfaction, for a little Mona Lisa smile plays around her lips. Eventually she decides to straighten up the dressing room which Margo has left in chaos. She puts the dressing table in order and then she picks up Margo's stage shoes. She notices the script lying in disorder on the floor. She retrieves it and settles down to serious study of the script. The lights black out. A spot picks up Margo, C.)*

MARGO.   *(Speaking to audience directly.)* It's funny about playwrights and actresses! You just saw Lloyd and me have a terrible fight. I don't really understand why it was so vicious. The truth is that we're natural enemies. I'm the cat; he's the dog. And yet we're tied together like a pair of Siamese twins. One can't function without the other.

People have said to me that I could walk on the stage and read the telephone book, and they'd be fascinated. It's a nice compliment to my ego and I'm flattered but deep down in my cat-like instinct, I know it isn't true. Before I got through the A's in that book, I'd hear snores all over the theater. They also say to me, "Oh, Miss Crane, you say such funny things." They forget that someone with more talent and wit than I have, has written down those amusing things for me to memorize. I can't even write a letter. It's a struggle for me to write a note that says "Thanks for the flowers."

That's the difference between a creative talent and an interpretive one. Without me those brilliant, funny words that Lloyd dreams up, would be as dead as if they were engraved on a tombstone. I bring them to life. Unfortunately, a dozen other actresses could do the same thing. I could be replaced. But no one can replace the playwright. I think that's why I treat them so badly. I belittle them and give them a very hard time. I think I do it because inside I'm really full of envy and jealousy. Their talent, if it's really good, will be printed in books like Oscar Wilde or Shakespeare and it will be put into libraries and live forever, while my talent, no matter how good, will die with me. It will live on, only a short while, in the memories of the people who have seen me act and who will someday, follow me to the grave. *(The lights black out as she disappears. They come up on Karen's library. Karen is seated alone, watching television. The audience cannot see the TV screen since the set faces into the room, its back being against the imaginary fourth wall. Karen is dressed as we saw her in her last narration, ready to go out to dinner. We hear classical music coming from the TV. After a moment or so, Lloyd enters. He has simmered down somewhat, thanks to imbibing a few drinks. Karen jumps up and turns off the TV.)*

KAREN. Darling, where *have* you been? Do you realize it's nearly half-past eight? Were you with Margo all this time?

LLOYD. I certainly was not. I've been propping up Sardi's bar getting loaded.

KAREN. *(With a flash of instinct.)* Uh-huh! She doesn't like the play!

LLOYD. Like it? She loathes it. Won't play in it. That's all.

KAREN. What about Clement?

LLOYD. Apparently he *does* like it. Will give me a production — without Margo.

KAREN. Then it's not the end of the world. Why are you so upset?

LLOYD. Without her, it won't last a day. You know that. I know that. She knows that. Boy, does she know it. She kept throwing it up at me. That's why I had a few doubles in Sardi's.

KAREN.   No wonder you're not seeing things straight. The fact that Clement will produce it without Margo should prove to you that he has confidence in you as a playwright. That's very gratifying.

LLOYD.   I'm being realistic. Without his egocentric harpy of a wife there won't be any box office advance and no parties. We could close the night we open.

KAREN.   That's being terribly pessimistic. Clement will have to get another star.

LLOYD.   So far he hasn't anyone in mind. Let's face it, Karen. This part has been specially tailored for Margo. Without her, everything's if, if, if. But that's not the worst thing. We had a ghastly row. We hurled insults at each other like a couple of polecats.

KAREN.   *(Ruefully.)* Hmmm.... It's going to be a pleasant weekend. I can see that.

LLOYD.   Don't worry. She's not coming. She sent you her sympathy for having married an incompetent hack.

KAREN.   *(Worried.)* Lloyd, tell me, is this a *serious* row?

LLOYD.   It's a split as wide as the Grand Canyon. We'll never make up.

KAREN.   *(Firmly.)* I refuse to let that happen. It's — unthinkable. It's just a storm in a teacup of temperament. I'm truly fond of Margo. And, at heart, she's devoted to you. You get on the phone and apologize to her this minute.

LLOYD.   *She's* in the wrong. She's let me down. After all the artistic sacrifices I've made for her. After all the time I've spent on this new opus.

KAREN.   You can call her in her dressing room. There's still ten minutes to curtain time.

LLOYD.   *(Sulkily.)* Why shouldn't she apologize to me?

KAREN.   Because she's a lady.

LLOYD.   Ha! That's the funniest thing you've ever said.

KAREN.   *(Dialing.)* I'm getting her number for you. You can behave like a gentleman, even if Margo isn't a lady. Now tell her you're sorry. That you lost your temper because you were so disappointed she wouldn't play the part. And say I insist on taking her to the country tonight as we planned.

LLOYD. (*Stubbornly.*) God-damn it, I won't do it!

KAREN. You've got to do it. If you don't apologize to Margo, Clement may never do your play. Are you going to throw a whole production down the drain because of your silly pride? (*Listening to the phone.*) It's ringing. Now get on the wire and eat crow.

LLOYD. (*Taking the phone savagely.*) It's more like swimming in bile. (*You hear the telephone ringing on the other side of the stage and the lights come up over there. Both rooms are now lit. Margo is in her first act dress putting the finishing touches to her hair. Eve stands by, holding a powder puff. Clement is sprawled on the chaise lounge, a drink in his hand. There is a suitcase beside the chaise lounge. The phone is ringing.*)

CLEMENT. You can't go on being mad forever, Pussycat. I'll talk to Lloyd from Chicago and smooth it over. Don't forget I want to do that new play of his even without your sterling presence. I have an instinct it'll make you and me a lot of money.

MARGO. What do we need money for? To support the government? I'll never speak to that unspeakable skunk again. (*To Eve.*) Answer the phone.

CLEMENT. You could have buttered him up a little, for my sake. Told him I think he's written a fine play.

MARGO. Why should I butter up a sour muffin?

EVE. (*Into phone.*) Miss Crane's dressing room.

LLOYD. (*Into phone — in his library.*) Hello, Eve. Put the First Lady of the Theatre on the phone.

EVE. (*Into phone.*) Just a minute, Mr. Roberts. I'm not sure she'll be able to talk to you. It's almost curtain time. (*Putting her hand over the mouthpiece.*) It's him, Miss Crane.

MARGO. I gathered that. Tell him to go to hell.

CLEMENT. You'll do nothing of the kind. Give me that phone. (*Eve hands Clement the phone, and gets out of the way. Clement and Lloyd now converse through their respective instruments.*) Hello, Lloyd. Clem speaking.

LLOYD. Hello, Clem. I wanted a word with Margo for a minute. You know we had a row?

CLEMENT. So I've been told.

LLOYD.   I bet you have! Anyway — I'm sorry! She got under my skin. So I said a lot of things I didn't mean. I'd like to tell her that personally.

CLEMENT.   That's big of you, Lloyd. I'm delighted you've called. Margo will be glad too. She's been in floods of tears about the whole thing.

MARGO.   *(Sotto voce.)* Tears! All I want to do is spit at him —

LLOYD.   Gosh! I *am* glad to hear that. I was afraid she'd never speak to me again.

CLEMENT.   You should know by now that Margo's flare-ups always die down in five minutes. She's just — what's the word — mercurial. *(Margo interjects a grunt that is almost a rude belch.)* The truth is she was bitterly disappointed your play didn't suit her. And I must confess that I agree with that. I'll put her on in a second. At the moment she's in the lavatory.

MARGO.   *(To her husband.)* Throwing up!

CLEMENT.   *(Puts his hand over the phone and speaks to Margo firmly.)* Stop interrupting! Talk to him. He wants to apologize.

LLOYD.   I was equally disappointed she wouldn't play in it. I guess that's what sent me up the creek.

MARGO.   *(Less adamant.)* I won't accept an apology.

CLEMENT.   *(Into phone again.)* I think you've written an excellent play. I'll get someone else to play the part. I've never failed yet. *(To his wife.)* Get on this phone and act like a lady.

LLOYD.   I'm so relieved you like it.

CLEMENT.   *(To Margo, again.)* He's one of the best writers in this town. I don't want him to take this play to another producer. *(Into phone.)* Without Margo I may be able to give you an early fall production. So the situation may have its advantages for you. Of course we've got to find a really good Cora.

LLOYD.   That's my great worry. Nobody would play it as well as Margo, in my opinion. *(Clement holds out the phone for Margo to take.)*

MARGO.   *(In an undertone.)* Now I think I really will throw up.

CLEMENT.   Here she is ... *(To Margo, loudly, so that Lloyd can hear through the phone.)* Darling — Lloyd's on the phone and wants to talk to you. *(Margo takes the phone with ill grace but speaks to Lloyd n a thin-lipped manner.)*

MARGO.   Yes, Lloyd, dear? What is it? I haven't long, you know. *(Lloyd covers the mouthpiece and throws in a remark to Karen, who is standing by listening anxiously.)*

LLOYD.   She's on the line hissing like a cobra. *(Into phone.)* Margo, darling! I'm sorry! Really I am. I'm shattered. I didn't mean those ridiculous things I said. *(He gives a hollow little laugh.)* Think of them as — dramatic license.

MARGO.   *(Into phone.)* I exaggerated too. I can't resist hamming it up. *(She echoes his meaningless laugh.)*

KAREN.   *(Whispering in Lloyd's ear.)* Tell her you adore her.

LLOYD.   *(Somewhat flatly, into phone.)* I adore you, Margo. You know that. I wouldn't hurt your feelings for the world. I was just devastated you wouldn't play the part. I lost my sense of values.

MARGO.   *(Her ego slightly restored.)* Actually we played rather an effective scene. A pity Eve didn't take it down in shorthand. You could have used some of that dialogue some day.

LLOYD.   Then you're not mad any more? You forgive me?

MARGO.   *(Cooing.)* Of course, you silly, sensitive stupid. *(She makes a face and sticks out her tongue at the phone.)* The truth is I adore you too. You know that.

KAREN.   *(Whispering.)* The weekend!

LLOYD.   By the way, Margo, about this weekend. Karen will never forgive me if you don't come to the country with us after the show.

MARGO.   Do you really want me?

LLOYD.   Clement's going to be in Chicago for several days, isn't he?

MARGO.   Yes. He's leaving for the airport in a few minutes.

LLOYD.   Then of course you must come. You can't be alone all weekend. It's going to be appallingly humid in town. You need the fresh air. We'll pick you up after the show as we planned.

MARGO.   *(Gratified, in spite of herself.)* Okay. I'll expect you. *(There is a knock on the dressing room door.)*

HARVEY.   *(Off-stage.)* First act, Miss Crane.

42

MARGO. *(Calling.)* I'll be right out. *(Into phone.)* They're calling the act. I've got to go. See you later. And, Lloyd, thanks for calling. Give Karen a kiss. *(She rings off.)* Did he eat humble pie! I bet Karen baked it.

CLEMENT. Probably. Karen's a smart woman.

MARGO. Are you pleased with me, darling?

CLEMENT. Very. You're my Margo. Thank you. *(Margo crosses to the door as Lloyd hangs up his phone.)*

LLOYD. *(To Karen.)* Satisfied? *(Karen nods.)*

MARGO. *(In doorway, to Clement.)* You *will* call me from Chicago?

CLEMENT. Of course. I'll be back Tuesday. *(He kisses her and she returns his kiss with a show of real affection.)*

KAREN. Was she gracious?

LLOYD. Charming was her middle name.

MARGO. So long. Have a good trip. *(She goes out to make her first entrance on the stage. Clement picks up his suitcase, ready to leave. Simultaneously with this action, Lloyd goes over to the cocktail table and lights a cigarette in silence. Karen watches him.)*

CLEMENT. Goodbye, Eve.

EVE. You certainly manage your wife marvelously, Mr. Howell.

CLEMENT. There's only one way to handle *any* woman. Put her in her place. *(He gives Eve a cool smile and leaves. The attention is now focused on Karen's library, though the curtains remain open on both sets. Karen and Lloyd converse, Eve does a little straightening up in the dressing room, then takes Lloyd's script out of a large handbag and settles down on the chaise lounge to read the last act.)*

KAREN. Don't you feel better now you've called her?

LLOYD. No. My inside feels like dry rot.

KAREN. I don't understand. Why is it so difficult for a man to apologize?

LLOYD. It isn't difficult, Karen, when he knows he's in the wrong. *I wasn't* wrong. She came into that dressing room with a chip on her shoulder. *She* was at fault. Having to apologize to her was like kissing her royal rear end. For once in my life I'd been true to my inner thoughts. I'd told her off and

I'd meant every word of it. I didn't want to retract one syllable. You don't realize what that little phone call did to my guts. *(Karen looks at him oddly. His words have both impressed and disturbed her.)*

KAREN. You're really angry, aren't you? With *me*, I mean.

LLOYD. It's not anger. It's something deeper. It has to do with — respect. You should have respected my feelings, Karen. You should have been on *my* side, no matter what it meant to our future. Instead, you insisted on expediency and I was weak enough to compromise. You've made me hate myself.

KAREN. *(Quietly.)* So long as you don't hate me!

LLOYD. *(Harshly.)* Let's skip any more analysis, shall we? *(He goes abruptly. She looks after him, bewildered and upset. Suddenly she picks up a cushion from the couch and kicks it across the room.)*

KAREN. Damn you, Margo. Damn you! *(For a moment or so she walks restlessly about the room, thinking deeply. Then she appears to come to a decision. She closes the library door and goes quickly over to the telephone; dials and waits. The phone rings in the dressing room. Eve puts down the script and answers it.)*

EVE. Miss Crane's dressing room.

KAREN. Is that you, Eve? It's Mrs. Roberts.

EVE. Oh, hello, Mrs. Roberts. What can I do for you?

KAREN. Are you alone?

EVE. Yes. Miss Crane's on the stage. There's no one here.

KAREN. Good. I want to talk to you. *(She hesitates a moment, then takes the plunge.)* Eve — how would you like to play Margo's part on Monday night?

EVE. *(Staggered.)* What *do* you mean, Mrs. Roberts?

KAREN. You know about the quarrel?

EVE. I certainly do. I had a ringside seat.

KAREN. Well, although they've apparently made it up, Margo's hurt Lloyd pretty deeply. I think Margo has to be taught a lesson. Let her find out that she's not as indispensable as she thinks she is.

EVE. I don't blame you. She was impossible. But how could such a thing be arranged?

KAREN. I haven't thought it out in detail yet. But I'm determined to find a way to make her miss Monday's performance. I know you'll do more than keep the curtain up. You'll be great. Perhaps when our star finds out, she'll be a little more tractable in the future. She'll be staying with us in the country as you know. I'll siphon the gas out of the car or something like that.

EVE. (Overjoyed.) Oh, Mrs. Roberts. What a wonderful revenge! Can I tell people that I'm going to play the part? A few agents, I mean. If they could see me it might help a lot.

KAREN. I don't see any harm. But you mustn't tell them it's a put-up job. Be very discreet. Even Lloyd has no idea.

EVE. Don't worry, Mrs. Roberts. I'll keep it a secret for the rest of my life.

KAREN. Harvey would let you go on, wouldn't he? I mean, he wouldn't close the show?

EVE. Don't worry about Harvey. He'll put me on all right.

KAREN. Very well then, Eve. It's a deal. This is your big chance. Make the most of it. (She hangs up. Karen also hangs up. Karen is extremely satisfied with herself. The lights black out on both rooms. After a reasonable pause, a pool of light comes up on the door framed by trellis work, D.L. When this door opens we can see the edge of a small occasional table with a telephone on it. In front of the door near the footlights are two comfortable full-length mat cushions. Margo is stretched out on the one nearer the center of the stage. Lloyd is squatting on the other one, beside her. He is wearing slacks and a sports jacket. Margo is wearing skin-tight stretch pants. A tea tray is on the ground between them. The light that shines on them should suggest late afternoon when the sun is in the process of sinking behind the horizon. The stage gets gradually darker as the scene proceeds.)

MARGO. (Sipping tea and munching crumpets.) I like my Julys to feel like July in Connecticut. Good and hot — like today. (She stretches luxuriously and glances upwards.) The sun must have gone under a cloud. But where's the cloud? Isn't it unusually dark? You are keeping your eye on the time, aren't you?

LLOYD. *(Glancing at his watch.)* Yes. Just after five-thirty. *(He too looks upwards.)* It certainly does seem a little dark. We should be leaving in about fifteen minutes. It takes exactly an hour and twenty minutes to drive to town. I'll have you safely in your dressing room at seven-fifteen.

MARGO. I wish I didn't have to go. Another day of this is what I need. *(Margo leans across the tea tray and takes Lloyd's hand.)* I can't tell you how glad I am you phoned me. I would have called you, eventually. I'm deeply fond of you and Karen. I always say to Clement, "My best friends are the Robertses." I'd never let anything come between us — not really. I don't know why I was so bitchy. I don't understand myself. I always overdo things.

LLOYD. That's why you're a great actress. You dramatize everything — including yourself.

MARGO. I seem powerless to do anything about it. It's as though a veil of madness falls over my mind. I can see through it but I'm in a sort of prison. Chained up and unable to move.... You really have forgiven me, haven't you? You know I respect you as a writer. I've loved everything you've ever written for me. I wish the new one suited me.

LLOYD. You're sure you won't reconsider?

MARGO. No. My personality is all wrong. When I know that, I smell a flop. You've written too good a play to wreck it with miscasting. *(Karen comes out through the door. She is wearing a summer cotton dress. She carries a muffin dish with her.)*

KAREN. More crumpets anybody?

MARGO. Hell, no!

KAREN. What about you, Lloyd? We've plenty of time.

MARGO. Does it seem dark to you, Karen? It does to me. Are you sure your clocks are right?

KAREN. We only have two. They're electric and they both say the same thing. I checked half an hour ago. *(Looking at the sky.)* Maybe it's going to storm — like last night.

MARGO. I don't understand that storm you've been talking about. I never heard a thing.

LLOYD. Neither did I.

KAREN. You're both disgusting. You must have slept like dormice. I was awake all night. The lightning was frightful. *(We hear the phone ring inside the house. Karen, who has been kneeling on the ground near the door, opens it and picks up the phone from the little table.)* Hello! Who is it? *(Pause.)* Just a minute ... *(To the other two.)* It's Harvey. He says it's ten to eight.

MARGO. *(Leaping to her feet.)* My God! I must get my things. *(She runs through the door.)*

LLOYD. Give me that phone. *(He jumps up and takes it.)* What do you mean, Harvey? All our clocks say five-thirty. We can't possibly get there until after nine ... even if I break every speed limit. Is there any chance of holding the curtain till then? *(A pause.)* What? Eve? *(A pause.)* Why the devil didn't you call before? If you' rung half an hour ago, we might have been able to hold the curtain. *(A pause.)* I don't understand that. We've been here all the time and we haven't had a call.

KAREN. *(Butting in.)* The phone was off the hook on the bedroom extension. Probably the cat up to his tricks. I just put it back a few moments ago when I went up to change.

LLOYD. *(Still at phone.)* Karen says the bedroom extension was off the hook ... *(A pause.)* Well, there's no more to be said. Give Eve our love and wish her luck. *(He hangs up. To Karen.)* Eve's going on.... This is the damnedest thing. I don't understand about these clocks.

KAREN. *(Innocently.)* It must have been that electrical storm last night. You know the power goes off sometimes.

LLOYD. It doesn't make sense. Even my watch is slow. *(Margo dashes in carrying a light summer coat and an overnight case.)*

MARGO. Come on. Let's make tracks. I'm ready.

KAREN. Relax, darling. You've got a night off. We couldn't possibly get there in time, even if they held the curtain a half hour.

MARGO. This is dreadful! I hate to disappoint all those people. This is only the third time in my career a show's had to close on my account.

LLOYD. *(After a pause.)* They're not closing, Margo. They're putting Eve on.

MARGO. *(Astounded.)* What? That's insane. You can't inflict a complete amateur on a paying audience. A girl who only walks through the lines in an empty theatre and will probably forget them when it's full.

KAREN. I don't think it's going to be that bad, Margo. In fact, Eve will do a lot more than keep the curtain up.

MARGO. What makes you say that?

KAREN. Well, as a matter of fact, Lloyd and I dropped in to an understudy rehearsal some time ago. Eve amazed us. She was very good.

MARGO. *(Not liking this.)* Oh, she was! You never mentioned that to me.

LLOYD. It just didn't seem important.

MARGO. So Eve is a girl of hidden talents! Well, no matter what you think about her ability as an understudy, I bet she'll make a mess of it when she stands in front of that black hole and sees all those ghostly faces.

KAREN. I wouldn't worry about it, Margo. What's one Monday night in July? Besides, you said you wished you didn't have to go back. You've got your wish. Let's relax and enjoy ourselves. Have some more tea.

MARGO. Tea! At this time of night? What I need is a good strong martini. For once I can behave like a human being on a weeknight. *(She goes into the house.)*

KAREN. Honey, go easy on Margo's drinks. She'll have one hell of a hangover tomorrow ... and, do me a favor, will you? Pipe down about the phone being off the hook, the clocks and so on — she's going to see through it.

LLOYD. *(Getting to his feet.)* See through what?

KAREN. You *are* obtuse! I thought you'd catch on.

LLOYD. We don't seem to be talking on the same wave length.

KAREN. Then tune in on mine. This was not an "act of God." It was an act of Karen Roberts.

LLOYD. (*Slowly.*) Are you trying to tell me that ...

KAREN. Yes. *I* planned it. *I* made her miss this performance.

LLOYD. (*Outraged.*) For God's sake, why did you do such a thing? Even tampered with my watch.

KAREN. Because *I* was furious with her too. I hated her for upsetting you. For humiliating you. Then, when you turned on me because I'd made you apologize, I felt she'd come between *us*. That made me really savage. I wanted to get back at her. Put her in her place. Show her that she wasn't so bloody important. That the play could go on without her.

LLOYD. What a damned fool thing to do! You women! You always go to extremes. Suppose Margo finds out about this? She'll never forgive you — or me. It's pure — perfidy.

KAREN. (*Emotionally.*) I repeat, I did it on impulse, because you were upset.

LLOYD. Impulse! You've had from Saturday night to Monday afternoon to think it over. That's no impulse!... Anyway, she must never find out. Never! Do you think Clement would produce my play if he knew you'd behaved like — Hedda Gabler? They'd both be finished with us forever. Why do you think she's getting plastered in there? It's because she can't bear the thought that somebody else is playing her part — even though it's only a nobody like Eve.

KAREN. I must admit she's very upset. I didn't think she'd take it so much to heart. She was saying all the weekend she wished she didn't have to go back this afternoon.

LLOYD. That was just talk. She only comes to life when she walks onto the stage. *Real* life is just something that has to be suffered until the curtain goes up.

KAREN. Well, there's nothing I can do about it now. It's happened. And I'm sure Eve will be good. Maybe I'll have given another dedicated actress her chance.

LLOYD. (*A sudden thought.*) *Eve* didn't know about this, did she? This wasn't a put-up job between you? (*Karen hesitates. Seeing how angry he is, she is now afraid to tell him the whole truth.*)

KAREN.   Oh no. No. Eve knew nothing.
LLOYD.   Thank heaven for that!... Karen, I may have been angry with you before. Now, I'm ashamed of you. No man would ever give his best friend a stab in the back like this. *(He picks up the mats and goes inside. Karen looks after him and bursts into tears. The lights dim out.)*

END OF ACT ONE

ACT TWO

The lights come on in the dressing room. The door is open and the applause has just about finished. Harvey ushers a man into the dressing room. This new character wears a slouch hat and is rather sloppily dressed. He has the look of a newspaperman, which indeed he is. His personality is somewhat sly.

HARVEY.   This is Miss Crane's room. Eve's using it tonight.

THOMPSON.   Thanks for bringing me backstage, Mr...?

HARVEY.   Harvey Marshall. I'm the stage manager.

THOMPSON.   I see.... This Harrington girl did quite well tonight, didn't you think?

HARVEY.   I agree. Why don't you sit down? She'll be here in a minute, after the cast have finished slapping her on the back. They were more nervous than she was. *(Thompson sits on the chaise lounge.)* I know you're on TV but what paper did you say you were from?

THOMPSON.   I'm with the *U.P.* United Press.

HARVEY.   *(Curious.)* Oh! Did you just happen to pop into the show tonight?

THOMPSON.   We had a tip. From the drama editor. I don't know how he got it.

HARVEY.   I saw the second stringer from *The Times* out there too. It's very funny. She didn't know she was going on till nearly eight o'clock when Crane didn't show.

THOMPSON.   Critics are at a loose end in the summer. Sometimes they drop in to see how a show is holding up — just for something to write about.

HARVEY.   Well, that's show business. Some actors get breaks, some don't. *(An indistinguishable babble of voices is heard coming along the corridor. Eve appears in the doorway. She calls down the passage, "Thanks, everybody," "You were all wonderful," "I'm deeply grateful," et cetera. Voices answer her and say "good night." She comes in, closes the door and sees that she has a visi-*

tor.) Eve, this is Mr. Thompson from the *United Press*. He wants a word with you, so I'll be on my way.... You did great, kid. Congratulations!

EVE. *(Aglow.)* Coming from you, Harvey, that means a great deal to me. I really do appreciate it. *(He pats her on the shoulder and goes out.)* What can I do for you, Mr. Thompson?

THOMPSON. *(Who has risen.)* I must add my congratulations to your colleague's, Miss Harrington. You were superb.

EVE. Won' t you sit down? Do you mind if I take off my makeup? I have a date. *(Thompson sits down again on the chaise lounge and Eve removes her stage makeup at the table during the following scene. Thompson takes a notebook from his pocket and makes notes.)*

THOMPSON. Go right ahead.... Tell me, Miss Harrington, how long have you been in New York?

EVE. About a year. Why do you ask?

THOMPSON. I want this interview with you for my column. It's syndicated all over the country. It's called "Broadway Charade." I'm going to head this "Birth of a Star." Not particularly original but true things never are.

EVE. You really think I could be a star?

THOMPSON. You certainly twinkled out there tonight. Tell me, how did you get this job?

EVE. I work for Miss Crane as a secretary.

THOMPSON. The stage manager mentioned that you were a fan of hers — used to hang around the stage door night after night. One of those fanatic kids who goes to a show again and again.

EVE. *(Smiling wickedly.)* Well, it's partly true. I did see the play quite a few times. You see, I was never a real fanatic about Miss Crane. I admire her, of course. Who doesn't? But I've always wanted to be a Broadway actress. I've acted in rep in the Middle West. I knew you had to get someone to take an interest in you; so I pretended to be an ardent admirer of Miss Crane to attract her attention.

THOMPSON. *(Flatteringly.)* In other words, you did a little off-stage acting. That was very astute of you. Tell me more.

EVE. Well, I persuaded a friend of hers to introduce me

to her. Then I became her secretary.

THOMPSON.   How did you wangle that?

EVE.   Oh, I dropped a few hints.

THOMPSON.   And then you finagled yourself into the understudy. *(Laughing amiably.)* You really fooled her, didn't you?

EVE.   I wouldn't put it like that. I sort of edged my way in when I saw an opportunity. I was determined to get my foot in a New York stage door somehow. I don't have to tell you that to get anywhere in this world you have to have influence — know the right people.

THOMPSON.   Well, marrying the boss's daughter has always been the fastest way to get to the top.

EVE.   Had you seen the play before?

THOMPSON.   *(Subtly leading her on.)* Yes. I was here opening night. What surprised me was that I was really emotionally moved tonight, which I don't remember happening before. The whole situation seemed to be more believable. Maybe age has something to do with it.

EVE.   Well, I don't want to be quoted, but Margo really is much too old for Elizabeth. Oh, she's a superb technician. There's nobody like her. But technique isn't everything. It's all on the surface. Elizabeth is only twenty-five and I'm twenty-five so I didn't have to *act* twenty-five. I could really feel it. That makes for reality. I think one of the great faults of the theatre today is the "Big Name" system. They put older actresses like Miss Crane in roles that should be played by actresses of my age. That may be good business but it doesn't make for truth in the theatre.

THOMPSON.   That rather sounds as if you're a method actress, Miss Harrington.

EVE.   *(Now wound up.)* I think all actresses of talent have their own method. I believe a part should be played from the heart; not from the head. Tonight I tried to think myself into the soul of this girl. I've studied Miss Crane a lot, naturally. Off the record, it seems to me as if you can predict exactly what she's going to do next. Acting should be more — adventurous. One should live dangerously in one's part. But within the framework of the play, of course. One should respect the author. One shouldn't rewrite his lines. Miss Crane does that all the time. I don't believe in it. I think the whole *art* of acting is to bring the written lines to life. To me, an author's text is sacred.

THOMPSON. You mean, Van Cliburn doesn't change Tchaikovsky's score?

EVE. Exactly.

THOMPSON. And that's what Miss Crane does?

EVE. It's the old-fashioned method of acting she's accustomed to.

THOMPSON. *(Lightly.)* In other words, she's a ham.

EVE. *(Coyly.)* Oh, you are awful! You know that's not what I'm saying. But I do think that sometimes a star lives on her reputation after her art's gone a little stale.

THOMPSON. *(Still fishing.)* The general opinion is that Miss Crane keeps her youth surprisingly well. I suppose that's all stage illusion.

EVE. Well, she does have a wonderful ingenue figure — thanks to dieting and massage of course. And stage makeup does wonders. She's an artist at that. Then special pink lighting helps create an impression of youth. *(There is a knock at the door.)* Come ... *(Bert Hinkle blows into the room. He is a smooth, well-fed theatrical agent who is constantly seen around town with beautiful women — mostly his clients. Margo Crane is one of his big moneymakers.)*

HINKLE. Well, young lady, you certainly left your typewriter behind you this evening.

EVE. Why, Mr. Hinkle! How marvelous of you to come! May I present Mr. Thompson of the *United Press?* Bert Hinkle.

HINKLE. We know each other. Hello, Thompson.

THOMPSON. *(Nodding.)* Now that you've put in an appearance, I know Miss Harrington is on her way up. *(To Eve.)* The biggest agent on Broadway doesn't bother with understudies unless it's ten percent worthwhile.

HINKLE. And you don't bother with understudies unless you smell a story. Right?

THOMPSON. *(Rising.)* Right! Miss Harrington is extremely

articulate. I think I've got enough material for half a dozen stories. *(To Eve.)* I'll leave you to Hinkle now. Take my advice. Play hard to get. I'll send you a copy of my column for your scrapbook.

EVE. Thank you so very, very much. I know what publicity can do for my career. I'm deeply grateful.

THOMPSON. Not at all. You're a godsend. I didn't have an idea for tomorrow's column till five minutes ago. *(Nodding to Hinkle.)* Good night, Hinkle. Miss Harrington! *(He leaves.)*

HINKLE. Old "Tally-ho" Thompson's fantastic. Trust him to get on your trail.

EVE. "Tally-ho." Why do you call him that?

HINKLE. It's his official nickname, because he has a nose for a story like a hound dog. And he can be as vicious as that animal when he corners his quarry. He's torn some of my clients to shreds. I hate his guts.

EVE. He was extremely nice to me — most flattering and sympathetic.

HINKLE. He would be. That's his technique. I hope you were discreet.

EVE. Oh, I just talked about myself. And acting.

HINKLE. Good! The right kind of an interview with Thompson can do a lot for you. He's very powerful.... What's the matter with Margo? I tried her apartment and got no answer.

EVE. It's nothing serious, Mr. Hinkle. She's up in the country with the Robertes. We don't know what happened yet. Probably something she ate.

HINKLE. I doubt it. That dame can digest rocks.... Tell me, how did you know in time to phone my office?

EVE. *(After a pause.)* I have a confession to make. I didn't know. I took a chance. The stage manager had a call this morning that she wasn't feeling well. He told me I might have to go on. I wasn't actually certain until eight o'clock.

HINKLE. I'm glad I saw you. You have a definite future, Eve. Both for the stage and films.

EVE. Do you mean that?

HINKLE. I wouldn't say it if I didn't. Of course, following someone isn't the same as creating a part. The main thing is that you have personality — a plus quality that's all your own. I think I can do a lot for you.

EVE.   How marvelous!

HINKLE.   I thought we might go across to Sardi's and talk about it. And we might drop in to the Rainbow Room for a dance on the way home.

EVE.   This evening?

HINKLE.   Why not? Did you have any plans?

EVE.   Nothing that I can't switch to some other time. *(With a flirtatious look.)* I'd love to have you handle me. I'm not going to take Mr. Thompson's advice and play hard to get. *(There is a knock on the door. Harvey opens it and comes in.)*

HARVEY.   Ready?

EVE.   Harvey, you've met Mr. Hinkle, Miss Crane's agent?

HARVEY.   Sure. Nice to see you, Mr. Hinkle. Did you catch Eve's performance tonight? Wasn't she great?

HINKLE.   Extremely good. I'm just taking her out to Sardi's to celebrate.

HARVEY.   *(With a look at Eve.)* Oh ...

EVE.   *(Returning his look.)* I'm hoping Mr. Hinkle will take me on as a client, Harvey. You understand what that could mean to my career?

HARVEY.   *(With irony.)* I understand. I understand very well.

EVE.   Mr. Hinkle. I wonder if you'd mind waiting over at Sardi's for me? I have to change and I'm sure Harvey has a few notes for me.

HINKLE.   Of course. I'll get a table. Take your time. I'll order some champagne. You'll need to unwind.

EVE.   That's very thoughtful.

HINKLE.   Nice to have seen you, Harvey. Don't keep her too long. *(He goes.)*

HARVEY.   I thought you were going to unwind with me.

EVE.   *(Getting out of her dress.)* That was before Hinkle showed up. You know what his interest could do for me.

HARVEY.   Sure. I get it. I can recognize a brush-off when I see one.

EVE.   There's no need to speak to me in that tone. You've

nothing to complain about. I've repaid you in good measure for what you've done for me.

HARVEY. And now it's Bert Hinkle's turn! *You* step up the ladder and *I* walk underneath it. *(He snaps his fingers.)* Just like that!

EVE. There was never anything permanent about our relationship. You were always very clear about that. After all, you *are* married!

HARVEY. *(Sneering.)* My God, I really bit into a wormy apple.

EVE. What do you mean by that remark?

HARVEY. You're rotten all through, Eve. You'll come to a bad end — up in lights with the other tarts. *(She slaps his face tartly.)*

EVE. How dare you say that to me?

HARVEY. *(Massaging his cheek.)* You know, now I come to think of it, something very screwy went on here tonight. I only told you you might have to go on at eight o'clock. So, how is it that Hinkle turned up here? And "Tally-Ho" Thompson? Not to mention a dramatic critic — from *The Times* too!

EVE. *(Frowning.)* Don't worry about things that don't concern you, Harvey.

HARVEY. *(Resigned.)* Okay! I guess I'd better pick up my pants and go. I should have known better than to mix pleasure with business. They curdle. *(He crosses to the door.)*

EVE. *(Stopping him.)* Harvey — don't think I haven't been fond or you. It's silly to have hard feelings, particularly as we have to go on working together. Let's be sensible about this. As they say in the theatre, "the tour's over. It was fun while it lasted."

HARVEY. And as they said in *Born Yesterday* — "drop dead!" *(He goes out and slams the door. The quarrel seems to have left Eve completely untouched. By now she has finished putting on her street attire. She studies herself in the mirror, gives her hair a final combing, then picks up her purse and crosses the room with her head high. After a final look around, she snaps off the lights and goes out, full of confidence in her future. The lights go down. They come up on Karen's apartment. The women are wearing the clothes they wore in the country.)*

MARGO.   It took much longer than an hour and a half to drive from Connecticut. I'd have missed another performance if we hadn't left early.

KAREN.   We usually don't have to cope with rush hour traffic. It's only six, Margo. You've got plenty of time. Just relax. I'll warm up the food. You must eat something.

MARGO.   Well, go easy on it. I never eat much before a performance. You know that.

KAREN.   A little pasta won't hurt you. It's a great takeout place. The best in the neighborhood.

MARGO.   *(Settling into a chair.)* Lloyd's taking a long time to get a paper. I should have gone home but I didn't like the idea of walking into an empty house with only Leila there ... I couldn't believe it when Harvey called and told you Eve got a notice. What do you suppose a critic was doing wandering around on a Monday night seeing a show he'd seen before. Even a second stringer.

KAREN.   *(A little too casual.)* Probably just an accident. They don't have anything much to do in July ... I'll put the dinner on. *(She goes out.)*

MARGO.   When Clement gets back from Chicago, he'll be amazed. He's at The Palmer House. I'll call him after I've read it.

KAREN.   *(Calling.)* I'm sure it's just a few lines. Something like "An understudy went on for Margo Crane last night." They're short of news this time of year. *(Lloyd comes in. He carries one newspaper.)*

LLOYD.   I couldn't get *The Times.* Completely sold out. But I've got the tabloid Harvey mentioned.

MARGO.   Give it to me.... This is the one that carries Tally Ho. *(She looks for the column.)*

LLOYD.   Karen, come in here, we've got Tally Ho. I can imagine what he has to say about my play without Margo in it.

KAREN.   *(Coming in.)* The dinner's warming up!

LLOYD.   Read it out loud, Margo.

MARGO.   Here he is ... *(She takes a pair of glasses out of her purse.)* ... My God! The headline is "Birth of a Star" and underneath there's a subtitle that says "Broadway celebrity bamboozled by understudy." Listen! *(She reads.)* "A bright new talent mushroomed in Shubert Alley last night when an unknown girl, Eve Harrington, stepped into Margo Crane's role in 'The Golden Circle.' She was so magnificent that I took myself backstage after the show to have a few words in person with this artful young actress." *(She looks up.)* What do you think of that? He's really flipped!

KAREN.   Nobody reads Tally-Ho Thompson.

MARGO.   You know that's not true, Karen. The whole damned town reads him. He's today's Winchell and just as powerful.

LLOYD.   Go on, Margo.

MARGO.   *(Reading again.)* "I found Miss Harrington singularly articulate and out-spoken. She told me that she owed her present opportunity to the fact that she had literally sneaked her way through the stage door by pretending an adoration of Miss Crane's talent with the sole aim of being her understudy." *(She stops.)* Remember that night in my dressing room, Karen, when you persuaded me to let her come backstage? This is all your fault.

KAREN.   Oh, please don't blame me, Margo. We were all taken in.

MARGO.   Clement wasn't. He warned me about her. He can see through any woman.

LLOYD.   Is there more?

MARGO.   Plenty. *(She goes back to the paper.)* "Miss Harrington was equally frank on the subject of Miss Crane's acting. If I may quote the lady she said, 'Miss Crane is no longer an ingenue even if she thinks she is. Actually, she's a synthetic concoction of tight girdles and heavy makeup, drenched in pink lights.' " *(Margo stops.)* How can she say a thing like that? Lloyd, read the rest. I can't see it. My eyeglasses are getting blurred. *(She hands him the paper.)*

LLOYD.   Where is it. Oh, here! *(He reads.)* " 'She's living on her reputation. Furthermore, her memory is failing.'"

MARGO.   That's not true. I can remember Peter Rabbit word for word.

LLOYD.   " 'She mauls the playwright's work disgracefully. Basically, her art is a surface thing of stage tricks. It doesn't come from the heart. It isn't real.'"

MARGO.   *(Terribly upset.)* Nobody ever said that about me.

KAREN.   Don't read anymore, Lloyd. It'll upset Margo's performance tonight.

MARGO.   Don't be a fool, Karen. I'll give the performance of my life. And this isn't Tally-Ho speaking. He's quoting Eve. Go on, Lloyd.

LLOYD.   "To sum up, Miss Harrington seems to feel that actresses of Miss Crane's vintage should be put out to grass like old mares, leaving the field open to young fillies like herself. It was refreshing to hear her put into words what many of us have been thinking for a long time. Broadway desperately needs new faces. Fresh ones. And that doesn't mean film stars out of work. Well, Miss Harrington is certainly fresh." *(There is silence.)*

MARGO.   That's all?

LLOYD.   That's all. There's not a word about how the play went with this young filly in it.

MARGO.   You're lucky, Lloyd.... How can I ever live this down? Everybody will be laughing at me.... Calling me an old mare behind my back.

KAREN.   It'll be a one day thing, Margo. By the end of the week nobody will even remember it.

MARGO.   I'll remember it. I'll remember it. *(In tears.)* I don't mind what she says so much. But I do mind her turning on me. Someone I've helped. Someone I was genuinely devoted to. I feel like I've been double-crossed. Stabbed in the back.

KAREN.   You have been, dear. She's been most ungrateful.

LLOYD.   That's the understatement of the week, Karen. She's been a bitch.

MARGO.   What can I do? How can I get my revenge? Sue her for libel?

KAREN.   It's not worth worrying about, Margo. Everybody

will be on your side. You've got all the friends in the world. She doesn't.

MARGO. *(Pulling herself together.)* What time is it?

LLOYD. *(Looking at his watch.)* Twenty of seven.

MARGO. Can I use the phone?

KAREN. Of course, darling. *(Margo picks it up.)*

MARGO. I'm so upset, I can't remember my own phone number.

LLOYD. 326-5167.

MARGO. Thanks. *(She pushes her own number. She waits. Lloyd glares at Karen. She fixes herself a drink. It's a straight scotch. Into phone.)* Leila, it's me. Call the garage and get the car. Tell the chauffeur to bring you to Mrs. Roberts' building. I'll be downstairs waiting. You're going back to the theatre ... I can't explain now. I'll tell you in the car. And bring a butcher knife with you. I may use it.

KAREN. What are you going to do??

MARGO. *(Hanging up.)* I don't know. I may cut her tongue out. I know one thing for sure. Miss Bitch is out of my life from now on. *(She throws on a coat she was carrying.)*

KAREN. Margo, you'll have to wait ten minutes for the car. Let me get you a bite to eat.

MARGO. Forget it. I couldn't swallow anything. I'd throw it up. My ulcers are in absolute revolt. I really feel sick inside. *(She goes out slamming the door behind her.)*

LLOYD. What are you drinking?

KAREN. A straight scotch.

LLOYD. Fix me one. *(She pours one and hands it to him.)* You see what meddling with clocks got you into?

KAREN. Don't rub it in, Lloyd, please. I wouldn't have had this happen for the world. I feel terrible.... What's that smell? My God, I forgot all about the dinner. *(She starts out.)*

LLOYD. As far as I'm concerned you can put it in the garbage. My ulcers are in revolt too. I'm going out to the nearest bar and drink myself unconscious. *(He goes out slamming the door behind him.)*

KAREN. To hell with the dinner. *(She falls into a chair.)* Sometimes, I absolutely hate myself! *(She finishes her drink in one swallow as the lights black out. They come up on Eve, sitting at the dressing table mending a strap on one of Margo's girdles. The door is slung open and Margo stands there with blood in her eyes. Leila is behind her. There is a deadly silence for a moment.)*

MARGO.   What a touching picture! A fresh young filly taking a tuck in an old mare's girth!

EVE.   *(Standing up, alarmed.)* Miss Crane — please!

MARGO.   *(Ignoring her.)* Leila, come in and sit down. You may have to keep me from strangling this creature. *(Leila enters the room and sits on the stool in front of the screen.)* How dare you, you pie-faced little hypocrite! How dare you open your butter mouth and spew up all that crap?

EVE.   *(Stuttering.)* Miss Crane, I — I can explain.

MARGO.   You couldn't explain this cretinous column if you talked yourself into your grave. In my book you've committed the unforgivable sin. Ingratitude! What's worse, you've made me a laughing stock and gloried in it. Your kind should be exterminated — like vermin!

EVE.   Miss Crane, you're being unjust. You don't understand ...

MARGO.   I understand all right. You used me. You used me to achieve your own selfish ends. *(She seizes the girdle out of Eve's hands and flings it across the room.)* What a double-dyed idiot I've been! Clement warned me. He told me the night I hired you that I was making a mistake. But I laughed in his face. Now I won't be able to show my face in Sardi's for a month. Everywhere I go, people will be twittering behind my back, "There goes old Margo — the Mare of Broadway."

EVE.   Miss Crane, I never said that.

MARGO.   *(Not hearing her.)* Well, young lady, you've had your moment in the sun. Now *you're* out to pasture. You're no longer my secretary. You're no longer my understudy. You're no longer my dresser. Go to the box office and tell them to give you whatever you're owed. Get out of this room. Get out of this theatre. Get out of my life. And if I ever catch you hanging around this stage door again, I'll have the police pick you up for vagrancy.

EVE.   *(Changing her tune.)* Very well, if that's the way you want it. I'll go. I don't need your help any more. I've proved what I can do. A big columnist has called me brilliant. I'm on my way up. You should have heard that audience last night. Even your own agent was enthusiastic.

MARGO. *(Like ice.)* Bert Hinkle was here too?

EVE. He certainly was. He took me to Sardi's and then we went on to the Rainbow Room. We're on first name terms now. I have an appointment with him at his office tomorrow.

MARGO. That's very interesting: "Tally-Ho" Thompson, and Bert Hinkle! Who else turned up?

EVE. I don't know, but they were enough.

MARGO. You must have got on that telephone at eight o'clock and sent out an SOS to everyone in town. I don't see how you had time to make up!

EVE. *(Hitting below the belt.)* I don't have to put on as much as you do. *(Margo almost slaps her, but manages to retain her dignity.)*

MARGO. That's enough!... Let me tell you something, young lady. A theatrical career isn't made by one performance. An overnight sensation can be forgotten overnight. You may learn that I have a lot of friends in this town. Friends who know the meaning of the word loyalty.

EVE. What about *your* loyalty? You should be grateful to me, Miss Crane. I kept up the curtain last night and saved your husband a lot of money. But you're so jealous because I made a hit in your part that you can't bear the sight of me. That's why you're firing me. Wait till I tell my side to the papers. You'll see.

MARGO. *(Very quietly.)* You dare to say one word more about me to the press and I'll fix your career forever.... Now get out of my dressing room so that I can fumigate the place. *(Eve shrugs her shoulders, gets her handbag and scarf off a hook and crosses to the door.)*

EVE. Goodbye ... *(With a parting thrust.)* May I make a suggestion, Miss Crane? Why don't you retire? It's always best to give up while you're still on top. *(She walks out and slams the dressing room door. Margo sinks onto the chaise lounge, exhausted from the emotional strain. Leila comes over to comfort her.)*

LEILA. You certainly told her off, Honey. She's nothing but

a nothing. Put her out of your mind. She don't exist.

MARGO.   Oh, Leila, Leila! Wasn't she horrible! *(Leila puts her arms around Margo, who leans against her bosom and cries silently.)* Tell me — is there any truth in what she said? Am I slipping? Am I on the way out?

LEILA.   Don't be silly, Baby. You're the greatest. Pure gold. That one's just brass.

MARGO.   There was some truth in what she said. I do need pink lights.

LEILA.   She'll need 'em too some day. Unless someone kills her before she gets that old.

MARGO.   *(Grimly.)* That would be too much to hope for.

LEILA.   About them pink lights — There's only one way to meet old age. Look it in the eye. Accept it.

MARGO.   I don't think I've ever been so let down. I feel all churned up with bitterness.

LEILA.   She ain't worth disturbing yourself about. She's gone. Forget her. We all love you. Mr. Howell loves you. The public loves you. That's all that matters.

MARGO.   *(Pulling herself together.)* I wish I had your wisdom. *(She crosses over to the dressing table, sits and stares into the mirror.)* Bitterness shows in people's faces. I mustn't let that happen to mine.... Tell me, Honey, I don't look too bad for forty-five, do I?

LEILA.   Thirty-five, Miss Crane.

MARGO.   No, God-damn it! Forty-five. From now on, I'll look my birthdays in the eye. *(She dips her fingers into the cold cream jar and starts to smear it on her face. The lights black out. After a short pause, a spotlight reveals Karen standing D.L., still wearing the same dress.)*

KAREN.   *(To audience.)* When Eve left that dressing room she walked out of our lives. One of the first things that claimed our attention was Lloyd's new play. Since Margo wasn't going to play the female lead, Clement engaged a star for the principal male role, then we set about trying to find a suitable young actress to play opposite him. Whether she had a big name wasn't important. Clement and Lloyd began having auditions and these had been going on for about a month when Eve suddenly walked back into my life. *(The lights in the library come up. Karen walks with deliberation into the set, picks up a book on the cocktail table, sits on the sofa and starts to read. In a moment, Eve suddenly comes in the door.)*

EVE.   Good afternoon, Mrs. Roberts! *(Karen jumps from surprise, her book falling onto the floor. She stares at Eve as if she couldn't believe her eyes.)*

KAREN.   Eve! How the hell did you get in here?

EVE.   I knew this was your maid's afternoon off so I didn't ring. And I knew you were alone. I saw Mr. Roberts go out.

KAREN.   That doesn't answer my question. How did you open my front door?

EVE.   With your keys.

KAREN.   What?

EVE.   Don't you remember you gave me your keys when you and Mr. Roberts went up to Boston for the road company opening? So I could come in and feed the cat.

KAREN.   But you gave them back to me.

EVE.   Naturally. But I had them copied first.

KAREN.   Whatever for?

EVE.   I thought they might come in useful sometime. Like *now*. When I *have* to see you.

KAREN.   You've got a nerve — barging in here uninvited. I want you to leave at once.

EVE.   Mrs. Roberts, you're entirely justified in your attitude. But will you listen to me for just a minute. It's terribly important to me, please.

KAREN.   *(Giving in out of curiosity.)* Well, since you're here.... *Why* do you have to see me? What's so important? You can hardly expect me to be very friendly after what you did to Margo. The things you said to that horrible columnist were unforgivable.

EVE.   Mrs. Roberts, that's what's so unfair. I never said those things to that dreadful man. He twisted everything. I tried to explain this to Miss Crane but she wouldn't listen. She flew off the handle in one of her rages and threw me out.

KAREN.   Can you blame her? It was a scabby column.

EVE. I don't blame her for being angry, but I do blame her. for condemning me without a hearing. She wouldn't listen to my side of it. Injustice makes me furious, so I fought back — like your husband did. That only made things worse.... Anyway, Mrs. Roberts, I'm desperately sorry about the whole mess. I had no idea a newspaperman would do a snide thing like that. It was a terrible shock to me.

KAREN. If you're in the public eye, Eve, one of the first things you have to learn is to be careful how you handle the press.

EVE. I certainly learned the hard way. Because of one terrible mistake I've ruined my whole career. *(She bursts into tears.)*

KAREN. Oh, come now, Eve, you're a smart girl. It's not as bad as all that.

EVE. *(Through her tears.)* It is. Do you know what's happened to me? Nothing, Mrs. Roberts, nothing! After that big success and those wonderful notices I haven't been offered a thing. I've tried and tried. I've pounded the pavements until my shoes are in holes. I can't get a reading. I can't even get an appointment with an agent. I can't get past the secretaries in the outer offices.

KAREN. I thought Bert Hinkle was interested in you.

EVE. He was. But when I went to his office for my appointment he wouldn't see me.

KAREN. Margo might have done that. She was good and mad.

EVE. It's like that wherever I go. Doors are slammed in my face.

KAREN. This is a funny town, Eve. Some actors are in; some are out. There's an underground grapevine. Word gets around. "This performer or that one spells trouble. Avoid them like the plague." So they don't work.

EVE. Well, that grapevine's strangling me. If *you* don't help me, Mrs. Roberts. no one will. I hardly have enough money to buy food.

KAREN. That's ridiculous. You can always go back to being a secretary. Outside Broadway nobody gives a damn what you said about Margo Crane.

EVE. I know that. But if I work full-time in an office I have no chance to do the rounds. If I have to give up my career, I'll kill myself.

KAREN. Now, now, Eve, you'll do no such thing. Stop dramatizing yourself. And please don't cry. I'll loan you a little money if you're so hard up.

EVE. I don't want money, Mrs. Roberts.

KAREN. Then what do you want?

EVE. *(Eve stops sobbing, surprisingly quickly.)* I want to play Cora, in Mr. Roberts' new play.

KAREN. *(After a pause.)* You're crazy.

EVE. I'm not crazy, Mrs. Roberts. I've been studying the part for weeks. I picked up a script in the dressing room. I know I can do it. I *am* Cora.

KAREN. My dear girl — there's absolutely nothing I can do. Besides, as you well know, Mr. Howell is the producer. Do you think he'd engage you after the way you treated his wife?

EVE. If he thought I was the best actress for that part, he'd engage me — whatever he thought of me personally.

KAREN. I don't think that applies in your case. Margo would divorce him if he employed you.

EVE. In any case, the playwright has the last word about casting. That's in the Dramatists' Guild contract. That means Mr. Roberts could choose me if he wanted to.

KAREN. The producer and the author have to agree.

EVE. They *would* agree — if they heard me read the part. That's all I'm asking you to do, Mrs. Roberts. Get me a reading. *(Suddenly.)* It's not set yet, is it?

KAREN. No, but they're narrowing it down.

EVE. Please, Mrs. Roberts, you owe me this chance.

KAREN. I don't see that I owe you anything, Eve.

EVE. It was your doing that I went on that night. You arranged it. You thrust me into the limelight for your own personal reasons. But you didn't tell me how to handle myself. Now it might never have taken place. It's like a mirage. *(She starts to cry again. This time Karen makes no attempt to stop her.*

67

She moves about the room thoughtfully.)

KAREN.   Eve, I don't know what to say.

EVE.   Just ask Mr. Roberts to hear me read. What harm could it do?

KAREN.   I suppose it wouldn't do any harm. I guess you've learned a lesson.

EVE.   Indeed I have, Mrs. Roberts. I've cried my eyes out for weeks.

KAREN.   Well, Eve, dry your tears. I'll see what I can do.

EVE.   *(Bursting with gratitude.)* Oh thank you, Mrs. Roberts. Thank you. You're a wonderful person.

KAREN.   Go to the Circle Theatre, Thursday morning, at eleven. I'll tell Lloyd to expect you.

EVE.   Mrs. Roberts, you're an angel.

KAREN.   I'm nothing of the kind. I'm practical. The sole reason that I'm getting you this reading is because I think you *could* play Cora. If I didn't know you had the talent, you could sit here and cry yourself into a stupor.

EVE.   Mrs. Roberts, I promise you you'll never regret this.

KAREN.   I seem to have heard that remark before. I certainly regretted the last time I helped you.

EVE.   I may have let you down off-stage, but certainly not on. I *was* good, wasn't I?

KAREN.   I'm not thinking about that. I regret having told Lloyd the truth — that I'd contrived to have Margo miss that performance. It upset him very much.

EVE.   *(Obliquely.)* Does he know that I knew in advance?

KAREN.   Oh, no. I didn't tell him that.

EVE.   He's not still upset about it, is he?

KAREN.   Not upset, exactly. But he seems preoccupied all the time. He's with me physically in the room but his mind seems out of the window.

EVE.   He's probably worried about getting a good Cora.

KAREN.   I guess that's it.

EVE.   It'll be a hit. I know it. And I'm going to help make it one.

KAREN.   Don't count on getting the part, Eve. They're considering a very good girl. Vera Franklin. She'll be reading

68

again on Thursday.

EVE. I've seen Vera Franklin on stage. She's first class. But I'm better. *(She picks up her bag and starts to go.)* Thank you.

KAREN. Just a minute, Eve. I'll take my keys.

EVE. *(Comes back digging them out of her handbag.)* Of course. I assure you I'd never have used them again.

KAREN. *(Taking them.)* I'm sure you wouldn't ... *(She pauses.)* Not until you needed them.

EVE. *(With a giggle.)* You're so funny, Mrs. Roberts. I've always loved your sense of humor. *(She goes to the door and turns.)* I can't wait for Thursday. That's always been my lucky day. *(This time she goes. Karen looks after her thoughtfully, then takes a cigarette from a box on the cocktail table. She lights it slowly. Then picks up her book from the floor and opens it but she is no longer interested. She tosses it aside and sits staring ahead, as the lights dim out. A few seconds later the stage "work light" that we saw at the understudy rehearsal now dims up slowly. There is a chair R.C. underneath the light. A young girl is seated in it, reading from a script. She is about twenty-five years of age and a different type from Eve, both as to coloring and personality. She is simply dressed in a dark wool suit. Harvey is standing near her, also reading from a script. Behind him, in the right corner, is a prompt table. He makes no attempt to put any variation into the way he says the lines. The girl, on the other hand, is reading extremely well. Her name is Vera Franklin.)*

VERA. "Go to the hotel. Get car. Car to take me to Mexico City. Two o'clock. This afternoon. *Esta tarde.*"

HARVEY. "Si, Senora. *Comprendo* ... Senora, you are better?"

VERA. "Yes. I won't cry any more. Sometimes when you dig deep into yourself you unearth a lot of things. Obsessions — lies. They shouldn't stay hidden or they may fester until you die of them. Perhaps I'm like your volcano — your white-haired Goddess of the Winds out there." *(She makes a vague gesture with her arm.)* "I've been dead inside for a long time. Now I've erupted and come to life again. *Adios,* Carola. Forgive me." *(Vera walks a few steps to the right and looks off into the wings.)* "What a beautiful mountain you are! I feel as if I'm seeing you for the first time. My eyes have been opened in so many ways." *(After a moment, she closes the script and looks directly out front. Harvey withdraws R., to the prompt table.)*

CLEMENT. *(Coming down the aisle of the theatre.)* That's very good, Miss Franklin. Very good indeed.

VERA. Thank you, Mr. Howell. I could have done better. But it's difficult to read well in this dim light.

CLEMENT. We understand. The unions do everything they can to hamper actors. *(Lloyd also comes down the aisle and joins him.)*

LLOYD. It was an excellent reading.

VERA. Would you like me to do any other scene?

CLEMENT. No, not today. If I want you to prepare another scene, I'll tell your agent. I'll be in touch with him. Would you mind going through the ordeal again?

VERA. Of course not. It's a marvelous part. I'll read as many times as you want me to.

CLEMENT. Well, thank you very much.

VERA. And thank *you*. You too, Mr. Roberts. *(She goes over to the prompt table. Her coat is lying on it and her handbag. Harvey helps her on with her coat.)* Au revoir — I hope. *(She goes off R., out of sight.)*

CLEMENT. *(Calling up to Harvey.)* Who else is here?

HARVEY. Only Miss Harrington, Mr. Howell. She's waiting in a dressing room upstairs. *(Clement comes up onto the stage, followed by Lloyd.)*

CLEMENT. All right. Get her. *(Harvey disappears off right.)* I think we're wasting time. I can't believe Eve will be better than this Franklin girl.

LLOYD. I want to be sure, that's all. Karen was most anxious that I should hear Eve read, just for comparison if for nothing else. After all, I saw Eve at rehearsals. You didn't. When she went on in Margo's part she made a sensation. This part also was written for Margo. So it stands to reason Eve might be a strong possibility.

CLEMENT. So's this Franklin girl. What's more, she's a nice girl — something our former little friend is not.

LLOYD. Karen swears Eve's most abject about the whole thing. She swears that damned columnist twisted her words.

CLEMENT.   Well, I'm giving her the benefit of the doubt, aren't I? I vowed I'd never let the little bitch in the theatre again. But when you get stuck you can't be too fussy.

LLOYD.   I wouldn't care if Lizzie Borden played the part so long as she played it well. *(Eve is ushered onto the stage by Harvey from the R. corner. She wears a fall dress and no hat. She carriers her handbag, a small umbrella and the script.)*

EVE.   Good morning, Mr. Roberts. Good morning, Mr. Howell. *(Both men nod coolly. Harvey stands behind her, glaring.)*

CLEMENT.   Hello, Eve. Mrs. Roberts has prevailed upon us to hear you read. So let's get started.

EVE.   I'm very grateful to you. I appreciate this opportunity more than I can say. It's very generous of you — especially after what happened.

CLEMENT.   That's water under the bridge. I don't propose to waste time discussing it. *(He goes down the steps across the footlights and into the aisle. Lloyd follows him.)*

HARVEY.   Same scene Miss Franklin read, Sir?

CLEMENT.   *(From the aisle.)* Yes.

HARVEY.   *(To Eve.)* Act III, page 32. Your last scene in the play.

EVE.   *(To Clement.)* Is that all you want me to do? I've studied the whole part.

CLEMENT.   If you can play this final scene, the rest won't be any problem. *(Eve puts her handbag and the script down on the table. At the same time she puts her umbrella on the floor.)*

LLOYD.   Eve, I suggest you sit down on the chair under that horrible working light. Cora should be seated at the start of this scene. She's just finished a letter at her desk. Get up and walk about, if you feel like it, as the scene progresses.

EVE.   Where do we begin?

HARVEY.   With the maid's line, "I no understand, Senora. You sick? *Necesito un doctor?" (Eve closes her eyes for a moment, concentrating very deeply so as to get into the mood of the scene. She holds the script but doesn't look at it. During this pause the two men go to the back of the theatre.)*

EVE.   "No, Carola. I don't need a doctor, I *know* what's wrong with me. My mother once gave me some advice. She thought it was good. But it was bad — bad! It planted something in my mind that has ruined my marriage. She said that no decent woman would so lower herself as to *enjoy* sex — that only immoral women indulged those sort of feelings.... When I married my husband I was still untouched. I was in love and that made it possible to submit. But that's all it was — submission ..."

HARVEY. "Senora — you speak too fast. I not understand nothing. Nada!"

EVE. "Of course you don't, Carola. *Lo siento.* Anyway, it's better you haven't understood." *(She stands up.)* "Now, listen carefully. Go to the hotel. Get car. Car to take me to Mexico City. Two o'clock. This afternoon. *Esta tarde.*

HARVEY. "Si, Senora. *Comprendo* ... Senora, you are better?"

EVE. "Yes, I won't cry any more. Sometimes, when you dig deep into yourself, you unearth a lot of things. Obsessions — lies. They shouldn't stay hidden or they may fester until you die of them. Perhaps I'm like your volcano — your white-haired Goddess of the Winds out there." *(She points to the back of the mezzanine.)* "I've been dead inside for a long time. Now I've erupted and come to life again. *Adios*, Carola. Forgive me." *(She looks back at the mezzanine again.)* "What a beautiful mountain you are! I feel as if I'm seeing you for the first time. My eyes have been opened in so many ways." *(She stops. She is no longer Cora but down to earth again. She takes a step forward, opens her eyes and looks out. Clement comes down the aisle, followed by Lloyd.)*

CLEMENT. *(Casually.)* Thank you, Eve. You've obviously worked hard on the part. You were quite good. Can you come back again Tuesday morning? Same time. I'd like you to read again. Study the second act scene where Cora finds out that her husband and the older woman are having an affair.

EVE. Then you think I might be right for the part?

CLEMENT. *(Briefly.)* You might be.

EVE. Oh, thank you, Mr. Howell. I know I can make a success in this part. I understand Cora's character. She's as clear to me as glass.

CLEMENT. *(Unimpressed.)* We'll make up our minds quickly. So you won't be kept too long in suspense. We'll tell you after Tuesday's reading. That will be all. *(Eve accepts her dismissal. She goes over to the prompt table and picks up her handbag and script.)*

EVE. Thank you for your courtesy, Mr. Howell — and yours, Mr. Roberts. Goodbye. *(She leaves. Clement and Lloyd go up onto the stage again.)*

LLOYD. She was wonderful. You'll have to admit it, Clem.

CLEMENT. Yes, she was excellent.

LLOYD. Well, what do you think now?

CLEMENT. I want to chew on it. One thing's clear. She and the Franklin girl are head and shoulders above all the rest.

LLOYD. What did you think, Harvey?

HARVEY. *(Cautiously.)* They're so different. The Franklin girl is more of a lady.

LLOYD. I agree. On the other hand, I feel that Eve has more sex appeal.

HARVEY. *(Unenthusiastically.)* I suppose she has that all right — if you go for her type.

CLEMENT. It's obvious you two don't agree. I'm on the fence. I think we ought to have a woman's opinion. Let's ask Karen to come to the reading on Tuesday. Since she's got fifty thousand bucks of her own dough in the show she's entitled to a say in the decision.

LLOYD. That's a good idea.

CLEMENT. Quite frankly, I don't particularly want to work with Eve. I dislike the girl personally. But I'll take her if Karen agrees with you that she's best for the play, artistically. Of course, I'll have one hell of a time with Margo.

LLOYD. Oh, don't you think she's simmered down about Eve by now? She doesn't usually hold grudges.

CLEMENT. She holds this one. But I think I can handle her. Anyway, I'll cross that bridge with Margo when we come to it.... Let's eat. At the moment lunch is more important than who plays Cora. We'll go out the front entrance....

Harvey, switch off that work light. We're through for the day. *(He and Lloyd step down into the aisle again and disappear into the darkness at the back of the auditorium. Harvey stubs out a cigarette in an asbestos tray on the prompt table, then carries it out into the wings. The stage is empty for a few seconds. He then returns for the chair under the work light. As he is carrying it towards the wings, Eve appears.)*

EVE.   Have they all gone?

HARVEY.   Yes. Did you forget something? *(Eve crosses to pick up her umbrella on the floor.)*

EVE.   This.... What was the decision? What did they say?

HARVEY.   *(With a sneer.)* So you forgot your umbrella? Deliberately, I bet. So that you'd have an excuse to come back and ask me that. In fact you carried it on this bright sunny day for the sole purpose of having something to leave behind.

EVE.   What of it? I asked you a question. What did they say?

HARVEY.   Why should I tell you?

EVE.   I was your girl once. That carries certain obligations.

HARVEY.   *(After a pause.)* All right. You've got a chance. It's between you and Vera Franklin. They're going to let Mrs. Roberts decide. She's got a lot of dough in the show. She'll be here Tuesday.

EVE.   Thanks, Harvey. *(She turns to go, then pauses.)* Harvey — what did *you* think? Did *you* like my reading?

HARVEY.   You were okay.

EVE.   Is that the best you can say? Did they ask your opinion?

HARVEY.   Sure. I had a swell chance to knife you in the back. But I didn't.

EVE.   That was very wise. Because I'm going to get this part, you know.

HARVEY.   I wouldn't count on it. You can't influence a woman like Mrs. Roberts. She's a very honest person.

EVE.   *(Quietly.)* Mrs. Roberts is going to pick me, Harvey. I was never so sure of anything. *(She turns on her heel and goes. Harvey takes up the chair and follows her. In a moment, the work light goes off. The stage is in darkness. When the lights come on again they reveal the D.L. corner, showing the flat with the trellised door. It is bright daylight. During the darkness, a small iron-work garden chair must be placed near the door, which is open. Karen is standing with her back to the audience. She has a pair of garden scissors. She is clipping some of the vines that intertwine the lattice around the door. She wears woolly stretch pants and a bulky sweater. After a moment, the phone rings. She leaves what she is doing, steps into the doorway, reaches over to the little table and picks up the phone.)*

KAREN.   Hello.... Yes, darling.... I'm planning to take the five o'clock train this afternoon. It's lovely here today. You've missed a glorious weekend. How's the cutting going?... Good! Did you work on that speech in Act Two that I think is too long?... Make it for eight o'clock. And don't forget to tell Susy we'll be dining out.... Nonsense. I'm the one who always remembers to lock up. 'Bye now. *(She hangs up and goes back to her task with the scissors. After a moment, Eve comes on R. and crosses into the light. She wears the same dress she had on at the audition, but it is now half hidden by a light fall coat. She has no hat and carries only her handbag. For a moment she stands watching Karen, whose back is turned to her.)*

EVE.   Mrs. Roberts ...

KAREN.   *(Startled.)* Eve! My goodness! Where did you spring from? *(She drops the garden scissors to the ground.)*

EVE.   New York. *(Pointing right.)* I've a taxi waiting to take me back to the station.

KAREN.   I suppose you're anxious to find out how you did at the reading? Lloyd was very pleased. You did quite well.

EVE.   I understand the part is between me and Vera Franklin.

KAREN.   I gather so. Lloyd said you two were unquestionably the best. So you have a chance.

EVE.   *(Coldly determined.)* I must have more than a chance.

KAREN.   I realize what it means to you, Eve. I'd like to see you get it. But I must be frank. If I think you're the best, I shall say so. If I think the Franklin girl is more suitable, I must tell the truth. So you mustn't be too depressed if you don't get this. I'm sure something else will turn up.

EVE.   Parts like Cora aren't written every year. I can't afford to let such an opportunity slip through my fingers.

KAREN.   I'm sure if it's your destiny to be a success, Eve, you will be. But one can't control such things. I've done all I can to help you. I got you the chance to read. Obviously you did well or you wouldn't be called tomorrow. But, from now on, it's in the lap of the gods.

EVE.   Not this time, Mrs. Roberts. The gods don't come into it. It's in *your* lap. I understand the decision is up to you.

KAREN.   *(A little coolly.)* You seem well-informed.

EVE.   I make it my business to be, Mrs. Roberts. A lot can happen at that audition tomorrow. For instance, I might not do as well as I did on Thursday. I might be nervous, knowing how much depends on it. I could be tired and not do my best. I dare not leave such things to — fate. I must know in advance that you'll choose me.

KAREN.   *(Sternly.)* That would hardly be fair to Vera Franklin, would it? As I explained to you, I must be impartial about this. I must be honest.

EVE.   *(With a covert sneer.)* Honest, Mrs. Roberts?

KAREN.   Yes. Honest. You must get it into your head, Eve. I can give you no promise that you'll be chosen.

EVE.   Since you're so determined to be "honest," I'll have to speak plainly. *(She picks up the scissors and fiddles with them.)*

KAREN.   Go ahead, Eve. This is very interesting.

EVE.   Your friendship with Miss Crane means a good deal to you, doesn't it?

KAREN.   So?

EVE.   I wonder how she'd react if she knew you deliberately made her miss that performance that night? Even your husband was annoyed with you for doing it. Think how much more angry Miss Crane would be to hear about it. She'd be outraged. She's always wondered how I managed to get the press there in time. It wouldn't be difficult to convince her that it was a prearranged stunt, if I told her that I'd called them *in the morning.*

KAREN.   Eve — this is blackmail. *(She sits weakly in the chair.)*

EVE.   You can call it what you like, Mrs. Roberts. That doesn't disturb me in the least.... May I bring up another point? What about *Mr.* Howell? How would he behave if he too learnt the truth? Shall I tell you? *(Karen doesn't answer.)* I think it might cause a real break between the four of you. He might even be so disgusted that he'd call off doing your husband's show altogether. That *would* be a shame, wouldn't it?

KAREN.   *(Stunned.)* You'd ruin the whole production if you couldn't get the part?

EVE.   I wouldn't hesitate for a moment. Don't let's waste time on words. *(She crosses to Karen and looks at her mercilessly.)* Now — do I get the part tomorrow? Or do I go straight from here to Miss Crane's apartment.

KAREN.   *(At her wits' end.)* They may not listen to me. Suppose I say I like you best and they still choose Vera? I can't put a gun to their heads.

EVE.   If, in spite of what you advise, they decide on her, then I suggest you tell your husband the truth. Let him know what I've threatened to do. He'll change his mind and choose me. I kind of sense that he liked me best anyway.

KAREN.   I *can't* tell him. I've already lied to him and swore you didn't know in advance you were going on that night. He'd never forgive me.

EVE.   Then it's all the more up to you to convince them, isn't it? They're undecided. They're in a mood to have their minds made up for them. You can do that, Mrs. Roberts. Men are puppets. You can pull the strings. You did it very ably before. Don't underestimate yourself. *(After a pause.)* Well, Mrs. Roberts, what's your answer?

KAREN.   *(With great reluctance, after a pause.)* So be it, Eve. If you keep your mouth shut, I'll do what I can to get you the part.

EVE.   *(Sweetly.)* I knew you'd see it my way.... Now I'll have to run along. I'm sorry I can't stay for lunch, but I want to get back home and work on the script. *(She hands her the scis-*

sors.) Be careful with these! I wouldn't want you to cut your own throat before tomorrow. *(She walks out of the light towards the R. and disappears. Karen continues to sit for a few moments in silence. Then she collapses in tears. The lights gradually dim out. When they come up again we are in Margo's dressing room in the theatre. Leila is alone in the room. An ironing board is up and she is busy pressing a dress. The noise of applause is heard off-stage. It rises and falls several times as the curtain apparently goes up and down. During this time Leila [obviously knowing that the show is over], closes the ironing board and puts it away behind the screen that masks the door to the bathroom. She hangs the garment she was pressing on a hanger on the back of the dressing room door as Margo comes in wearing her stage dress.)*

MARGO.   *(Delighted with herself.)* What an audience! They loved me. A real ovation. Did you hear that applause?

LEILA.   I heard.

MARGO.   Thank God I've done my last performance. I've loved this part but I'm glad to put it behind me. I'm tired of it. Still it's nice to bid "Elizabeth" goodbye to a full house.

LEILA.   I got a message from Mr. Howell. Came back after intermission.... He'll be in after he says goodbye to the cast.

MARGO.   Oh, the darling! Really sat through my closing night performance. Isn't that real devotion?

LEILA.   I don't see why you're closing. That audience is packed like sardines out there. You aren't even on twofers yet.

MARGO.   It's had its time, Leila. The advance is down to nothing. No point in losing money during August. You know what I'm going to do now until September? I'm going to one of those fancy Spa's and stop eating and start exercising.

LEILA.   What a grim idea! If you get any thinner, Mr. Howell will think he's in bed with a skeleton.

MARGO.   He'll be too busy with the new play to think about bed.

LEILA.   Who got the leading part in the new play?

MARGO.   They had the final auditions this morning. Clement told me it would probably be a girl named Vera Franklin. He says she's marvelous.

LEILA.   Harvey told me that bitch, Eve Harrington, was reading for it. I was surprised they let that piece of garbage in the theater.

MARGO.   Clem told me it was just a formality to please Mr. Roberts. Meant nothing. Clem says playwrights never know what they want. You have to cater to them to keep them happy. They worry all the time. And this part has been hard to cast since *I* didn't want to do it. I haven't talked to Clem today. He had a lot to do besides auditions. I'll find out to-night. *(There is a knock on the dressing room door.)*

CLEMENT.   *(Off-stage.)* Are you decent? Can I come in?

MARGO.   *(Calling.)* Of course, darling. *(Clement opens the door. He doesn't look happy.)* Darling, you were an angel to sit through the show. It was a good performance, didn't you think?

CLEMENT.   *(Kissing her.)* One of your best. You were really marvelous tonight. I thought to myself, "She's as good on the closing night as she was on the opening night. No embroidery!"

MARGO.   Well, I do my best to keep your direction the way you created it.

CLEMENT.   Leila, I want to talk to my wife alone. You can go home. We'll lock up.

LEILA.   Thanks, Mr. Howell. There's a late movie on TV that I want to see. I'll just catch it. Robert Redford's in it. I missed it the first time around. Bye-bye. *(She goes out, closing the dressing room door behind her.)*

MARGO.   What's so secretive that Leila can't hear it?

CLEMENT.   I like to have our fights in private. I know you're going to blow your top and I prefer that she be absent. *(After a pause.)*

MARGO.   *Eve* got the part.

CLEMENT.   I regret to say that she did.

MARGO.   *(Quietly.)* I can't believe you. *(Suddenly she is in a rage.)* How could you let this happen? How could you do this to me? You know how I feel about Eve.

CLEMENT.   How you feel has nothing to do with this.

MARGO.   It has everything to do with it. Giving that little snake a break! You've double-crossed me. Your own wife.

CLEMENT.   Don't yell! You'll scare the stagehands.

MARGO.   I hate you. I'll divorce you.

CLEMENT.   You'll do nothing of the kind. And you don't hate me. You love me. Now just simmer down. This is not my fault.

MARGO.   Of course it is. You're the producer. You have the authority. Why did you give it to her after the way she behaved to me?

CLEMENT.   I had to make a decision. Either give her the part or call the play off.

MARGO.   Then you should have called it off. How did you ever get in such a position?

CLEMENT.   Lloyd and Karen were against me. They were both set on Eve.

MARGO.   *(Furious.)* My two best friends were against me as well as you? I'll never speak to either of them again.

CLEMENT.   *(Patiently.)* This has nothing to do with friendship. It's a question of what was best for the play.

MARGO.   What was the matter with that other girl you raved about? This Vera somebody. You told me she was marvelous.

CLEMENT.   I thought she was but I was outvoted. I could have won over Lloyd, I think. But Karen was adamant.

MARGO.   What's she got to do with it? She's not the writer, or the producer or the director.

CLEMENT.   No, she's not. But she's a great deal of money. Fifty thousand dollars worth of money. She threatened to take it out of the show if I didn't use Eve.

MARGO.   That doesn't make sense to me. She hates Eve as much as I do. She was always on my side.

CLEMENT.   That's why I knew she was being truthful in her judgement. I knew she wouldn't select Eve without a good reason. She just thought Eve was better for the role. She said the other girl had no sex appeal. After all, Lloyd had written it for *you* and sex appeal is *your* middle name.

MARGO.   You're flattering me. You don't love me, Clement, or you wouldn't do this to me. *(She bursts into tears. Clement*

takes a handkerchief out of his pocket and hands it to her.)
CLEMENT.   Tears aren't going to work, Margo. You can turn them on like a faucet. I know you.
MARGO.   I'll never get over this.... Never!
CLEMENT.   Yes, you will. *(He pauses.)* Margo, you've got to put Eve and what she did to you, behind you, I don't like to see you holding a grudge. You're being vicious and revengeful. It's not good for you, darling. Eve is getting this part, only because she's talented and sometimes talent overcomes a nasty character. She's won this battle because she's *tough* and that's what you have to be, to be a star. She's as tough as *you* are. I'm taking you to Twenty-One to supper, and I don't want Eve mentioned again.
MARGO.   *(Pulling herself together.)* Okay, Clement, I suppose you're right. She's been like a worm eating away at my insides. I know I must blank that incident out of my mind. But I'm making *one* condition.... You don't direct this play. I don't want you breathing the same air as that bitch. You might catch something. Let Lloyd direct it. He's always wanted to do his own plays. And if he makes a flop out of it, he'll have nobody but his own wife to blame. She can lose her damned fifty thousand.
CLEMENT.   All right, Margo. I'll give in on that. I wouldn't let Eve or Karen or Lloyd come between us for the world. *(He takes her in his arms and kisses her.)* Talk about sex appeal ... maybe we should forget about Twenty-One. What do you say? *(The lights black out. A spotlight comes up on Karen. She speaks directly to the audience.)*
KAREN.   I'm happy to say that all went well. Eve stayed as silent as a mouse as far as I was concerned. And Lloyd had a great time directing his own play. He said Eve was the hardest working actress he'd ever seen. She even persuaded him to coach her in the evenings. The play turned into a smash hit and Eve became Broadway's newest star. Margo even went back on the opening night with Clement and congratulated her. Privately, I knew it was Margo's greatest performance. Time passed. The opening was in October. Now it was June. Eve was leaving the cast. Her agent — Bert

81

Hinkle's greatest rival — had got her a three picture deal in Hollywood. She was being replaced by little Vera Franklin, who hadn't had a job all season. *(Karen walks out of the spotlight as the regular lights come up in the dressing room. The door is open. One simple day dress that Eve wears in her play is hanging on a hanger. There are also two evening dresses hung up. One is a beautiful white one that Eve is going to wear to a TV broadcast. The other, a colored dress, belongs to Vera Franklin. Vera is being fitted into a day dress. Margo's former maid, Leila, is fussing with the hem.)*

LEILA.   I think that does it. It don't need to be too short.

VERA.   *(Looking at herself in the mirror.)* It's too bad it's not another color. I don't think this suits me.

LEILA.   They ought to buy you some new clothes. Makes you feel like a hand-me-down. *(There is the sound off-stage of tremendous applause.)*

VERA.   There's the curtain. You'd better get me out of this. She'll be wanting her room. *(During the next few speeches we hear the applause increase and die down according to the rise and fall of the off-stage curtain. Leila gets Vera out of the stage dress and into her own evening gown.)*

LEILA.   Be careful of those pins. You might scratch them pretty gams of yours. *(Vera steps out of the dress and stands in her undies. She has on a scanty undergarment and a half-slip.)*

VERA.   I'm so excited to have this chance tonight. Coast-to-coast on "Tally-Ho's" TV program! It's wonderful publicity for me.

LEILA.   *(With the evening gown.)* Step into this. No sense in mussing your hair before the telecast. *(Vera does so. Leila works on the hooks in the back.)* Don't kid yourself, dearie. They're not thinking of your publicity. It's the show.

VERA.   Oh, I know. I'm a very lucky girl. It's funny. Last October when I didn't get this part I was ready to kill myself. I'd done my best and I was certain Mr. Howell was crazy about me. I couldn't understand why they didn't give it to me. Well, better late than never, I guess.

LEILA.   It's all in the toss of the dice, Sweetie. You never know how they're going to fall. *(Vera is now dressed. Leila hands her a silk stole.)* My, you look a knockout. And I seen you rehearse. Don't you worry yourself. You're as good as her. Between the two of us, it's very strange to me that she got the part. Miss Crane hates her guts and Mr. Howell don't like her much either. In fact, if you wanta know, he put me in here to dress her because he wanted somebody to keep an eye on her. See that she wasn't up to any tricks. He don't trust her and since Miss Crane isn't working ... *(Eve comes into the room, dressed as Cora, so the above conversation comes to a halt. Eve wears a simple Mexican cotton skirt and a peasant type blouse. Hundreds of tourists buy them every year.)*

VERA.   Oh, Miss Harrington, I'm getting out right away. Mr. Howell told me to come back here and try on your first and second act dresses.

EVE.   Of course. *(She is very sweet and gracious to Vera.)* You don't have to go. Stay and talk. *(Leila now proceeds to get Eve changed.)* Did you see any of the performance tonight?

VERA.   I watched the first act. You were simply marvelous.

EVE.   I tried my very best — because it's my last performance. I didn't want to let Cora down. I wanted her to live as she's never lived before. I feel I'm shedding my skin — like a snake. I hate to leave. *(Lloyd appears in the doorway, dressed in a dinner jacket. He and Eve are obviously now very friendly.)*

LLOYD.   Hi, Baby! You were great tonight. Great! *(To Vera.)* How are the clothes? Do they fit?

VERA.   Minor alterations.

EVE.   Clement's a cheapskate. He ought to buy her new ones.

VERA.   *(Laughing.)* Please don't suggest that, Miss Harrington. If I couldn't wear these, they might get another girl.

LLOYD.   Mr. Howell's waiting out front in the car.

VERA.   Then I'll get out of your way. Four's a crowd in this dressing room. *(She goes quickly. There is a slight pause.)*

EVE.   She's a darling girl.

LLOYD.   *(Quietly.)* She'll never be Cora to me — after you.

EVE.   *(With a smile.)* You're prejudiced.

LLOYD.   When I remember how close it was, it seems a miracle we made the right decision.

EVE.   *(Lightly.)* It was the power of positive thinking. I *willed* it to happen! Well, I seem to be ready. I haven't time to take off my makeup. *(She twirls for him in her white dress.)* How do I look, Lloyd?

LLOYD.   What is it they say? White for purity? It suits you marvelously.

EVE.   *(Kissing Leila and slipping her a ten dollar bill.)* Goodbye, Leila. I'm going to miss you.

LEILA.   Thank your Eve. I'll pack your makeup and leave it at your hotel tonight. Good luck in Hollywood. We all expect you to win an Oscar.

EVE.   *(Demurely.)* I probably won't get the chance. They say it's fixed in advance. *(She throws her white mink stole over her shoulders and goes out with Lloyd. As Leila starts to pack up the makeup, she talks aloud to herself.)*

LEILA.   I bet she's the little bitch who can *unfix* it. The snake is headed for The Garden of Eden. *(The lights black out. They come up again on Karen's library. Karen and Margo are in the room. Karen wears a severe black silk dress. Margo is informally attired. Both ladies are well in their cups — not drunk, but definitely "high." A half-empty bottle of Scotch is on the cocktail table with a bucket of ice. Margo is mixing herself another highball. Karen is sipping one, slumped in an armchair. They are both rather loud and articulate, more than usual.)*

MARGO.   So I said to Clement, "I won't go to the bloody TV studio until they give her the Congressional Medal of Honor — posthumously."

KAREN.   I'm glad you decided to stay here with me instead.

MARGO.   Why didn't *you* want to go?

KAREN.   Because I'm not in the script.... What time is it? *(She studies her watch.)* Don't wanna miss this silly broadcast ... I can't read the face on my watch. It seems to have a double chin. *(She suddenly thrusts her arm in front of Margo's nose. Margo peers at it nearsightedly.)*

MARGO.   It's not eleven-thirty yet. Of course, I don't trust the clocks in your house any more.

KAREN.   Don't worry. We now run on TV time. I need another snifter. *(She pours a little more Scotch into her glass.)*

MARGO.   You'd better slow down, my poppet, or you'll see two Eve Harringtons on the TV screen. Believe me, one is quite enough.

KAREN.   One is too many. *(She raises her glass.)* To me — to Karen Roberts — the prize sucker. *(She downs her Scotch in one.)*

MARGO.   What's the matter with you tonight, Karen? You're not usually such a good drinking companion. Generally I have to get loaded all by myself.

KAREN.   *(With a funny gesture to the TV set.)* I've got a secret.

MARGO.   Let me in on it. What's a secret between friends? I'll only tell a few people.

KAREN.   This is a secret about Eve.

MARGO.   You can't tell me anything about that creep that would surprise me. *(Waving her arm.)* However — let's gossip about her. It gives us something to talk about while we're talking. *(Karen crosses, glass in hand, and sits very close to her, peering into her face.)*

KAREN.   Margo Crane — star of Broadway — you don't know the half of it.

MARGO.   I *do* know the half of it. So tell me the other half. *(Karen gets up unsteadily and weaves over to the bookcase.)*

KAREN.   Where the where did I put it? *(She peers at the books.)*

MARGO.   Where the where did you put what?

KAREN.   The report. I hid it some place.... Oh yes. I stuck it between *Lady Chatterley* and *Fanny Hill*, unexpurgated. *(She pulls some official-looking papers from between two books.)* Here we are. The Memoirs of Fanny Harrington — a report.

MARGO.   You're not making sense. What report?

KAREN.   *(Very confidentially.)* You have no idea what a good detective can dig up. Boy, oh boy!

MARGO.   A detective? Why? What for?

KAREN.   Just a hobby. I decided to blow some of the money I've earned from *When the Winds Blow*. I've had our little star investigated. *(She laughs a little stupidly.)*

MARGO.   Well, what's it all add up to? Do come to the point.

KAREN.   Well, this detective — the one I went to see — had an operative from his Chicago office make a little trip up to Wisconsin.

MARGO.   Wisconsin?

KAREN.   Yes. Don't you remember? Eve told us she came from Milwaukee. That was true. But it was the only thing she said that was. *(Reading from the report.)* "Eve Swanson was the *only* child of a Mr. and Mrs. Olaf Swanson."

MARGO.   She said there were six children!

KAREN.   A slight exaggeration ... *(Reading again.)* "Mr. Swanson died of heart failure when his daughter was sixteen. After a year, Mrs. Swanson married again. Her second husband was Eric Harrington.

MARGO.   I must be tight. Eve said *she* married a Ricky Harrington.

KAREN.   You're not tight. I am. I'm so plastered I can't read this. So I'll tell you the gist. *(She makes a violent effort to pull herself together. As she continues with Eve's story, her articulation becomes more normal.)* Eve had no husband. There was no accident. There was no jet pilot in her life. *(This statement sobers Margo somewhat.)*

MARGO.   My God!

KAREN.   Harrington was her stepfather's name. Her mother said that she had trouble with Eve the minute she graduated from high school. The first thing she did was to get a job in a summer stock company out there. She started as an apprentice, but it was the fastest apprenticeship on record. The manager took her under his wing.

MARGO.   *(Laughing.)* How chaste!

KAREN.   The regular ingenue was sacked. Eve got all her parts. Her mother knew what was going on. But she couldn't do anything about it. She closed her eyes. This went on for a couple of summers. In the winter she did work in a restaurant. Her stepfather's restaurant. She also worked on her stepfather. When her mother found out she was competing with her own daughter, she couldn't stand it any longer. She kicked Eve out.

MARGO.   Sounds like a Eugene O'Neill play.

KAREN.   Eve went on to bigger and better things, and men, in Chicago. This private eye checked all the business schools and found the one she went to. The owner said her bills were paid by a Mr. Russell Guest. He was married, a big shot in some advertising agency. God knows where she met him.

MARGO.   Maybe she was a Playboy Bunny.

KAREN.   Possible. Anyway, she worked for this Mr. Guest in the winter. In the summer, he gave her a leave of absence to play in stock companies around Chicago. She did a lot of work. She became an Equity member, under the name Eve Swanson. She didn't use Harrington until she came to New York. She joined the union again under that name when we hired her.

MARGO.   So that explains it. I always thought it was fishy how she stepped onto the stage as a supposed amateur and did so well.

KAREN.   She didn't come on to tackle Broadway until she was ready. Then she thought out a careful plan to break in fast.

MARGO.   But the whole story's fantastic. All that crap about her dead parents, her husband being killed, and sad, lonely widow! Why?

KAREN.   She thought out a role that would get sympathy and she played it to the hilt. Anyway, it worked.

MARGO.   It certainly did. And you've sobered me up. *(She grabs the report out of Karen's hand.)* Give me that. I want to read all the gory details. *(She starts to read with concentration.)*

KAREN.   You've only got a few minutes ... I think I've sobered myself up too. *(Karen fixes herself another drink and sips it pensively. The interest now goes to the other side of the stage. The lights come up on the right half of the stage. This area may now be presumed to represent a segment of a TV studio. "TALLY-HO" THOMPSON appears from the wings. He carries a high stool which he sets down behind the microphone. Vera, Clement and Lloyd, and, last of all, Eve, follow him. They too carry stools.)*

THOMPSON.   Bring your stool over by mine, Miss Franklin.

You appear first. *(She does so. The other three place their stools nearby and sit. He turns to them.)* When I call upon any of you, you'll replace Miss Franklin here. *(He then points to the audience.)* There are the cameras. But don't worry about them. Act as if they're not there. Just be yourselves.

VERA. I'm so excited.

THOMPSON. Relax, Miss Franklin. Look at Miss Harrington. She's as cool as a cucumber.

EVE. That's just a facade. You don't know what's behind it.

THOMPSON. We'll be on the air any moment. *(He looks out front again.)* How long have we got, John?

VOICE. *(Through microphone.)* About forty seconds.

THOMPSON. *(To the group.)* I take my cue from the floor manager. Watch me. As soon as I start talking, we'll be on camera. Try not to cough or sneeze.

VOICE. *(Through microphone.)* Twenty — seconds. *(The four people in the studio sit like frozen statues, staring at Thompson. In the library, Karen looks at her watch, then gets up and switches on the TV. She takes the report away from Margo.)*

KAREN. Here we go, Margo. That sweet Mr. Thompson is about to pollute the airwaves.

MARGO. I need another drink. All this hot air will give me a dry throat. *(She mixes herself a drink. Karen sits beside her. They both stare at the TV screen. The set is facing them. It may be presumed that what they see is happening R. Thompson makes a sign, then begins to speak directly out front.)*

THOMPSON. Ladies and Gentlemen, this is David Thompson speaking, bringing you "Broadway Charade," live from New York. This evening is especially important, because I intend to present what is known from coast to coast as the David Thompson Medal to the young actor or actress who has been most cooperative to the press during the past season. Who this is will be no secret to you since her name has been announced already in my syndicated column, "Broadway Charade," that appears in nine hundred papers in the United States. The winner is *Miss Eve Harrington....* However, before you meet this charming young lady — *(Margo blows a raspberry.)* I'd like to introduce to you a few of the people connected with the play, *When the Winds Blow*, in which Miss Harrington has made such a spectacular success. The first person is this pretty young lady on my right who, on this coming Monday night, will replace Miss Harrington. Miss Vera Franklin. Vera, say hello to the viewers.

VERA. *(Nervously.)* Hello.

THOMPSON. Tell me, darling, how does it feel to be stepping into such a wonderful part?

VERA. It feels heavenly. I'm the luckiest girl I know.

THOMPSON. *(Throwing her a curve.)* You'd have been luckier still if you'd got the part in the first place, wouldn't you? I understand you read for it. *(Vera hesitates, embarrassed at this reference to her defeat.)*

MARGO. What a lousy stinker!...

VERA. Of course, Mr. Thompson. But Miss Harrington plays Cora so magnificently that I don't carry a grudge.

THOMPSON. You're a very sweet girl.

VERA. The theatre's so much a matter of luck. One has to be philosophical about it.

THOMPSON. *(Slyly.)* Don't other things count besides luck?

VERA. Such as?

THOMPSON. Well — if someone takes a *personal* interest in you?

VERA. *(Coldly.)* That's an old-fashioned thought, Mr. Thompson. Production costs are so high these days that girls aren't cast any more because of — romantic attachments.

THOMPSON. In other words, sex has gone out of style in the theatre. I'm afraid you're an idealist, my dear.

VERA. I hope so.

THOMPSON. I'm sure you're going to be very good in the part, though it must be tough to have to follow Miss Harrington. *(Dismissing her rather abruptly.)* Now, Miss Franklin, if you'll take Mr. Howell's place, I'd like the viewers to meet the producer of *When the Winds Blow*.

VERA. Thank you. *(Getting off the stool. She and Clement exchange places.)*

THOMPSON. Ladies and Gentlemen, you've met this gentleman many times on my program. Clement Howell is one of the few Broadway producers who can read — that is to say, he knows a good script when he's handed one. He doesn't have to see it on the London stage first. He is also the husband of that great actress, Miss Margo Crane.

MARGO.   Thanks for the plug, Louse!...

CLEMENT.   Good evening, everybody.

THOMPSON.   Tell me, Mr. Howell, is this the first play you've produced without your wife in the lead?

CLEMENT.   Heavens, no. I did many plays before I met Miss Crane.

THOMPSON.   Why didn't you cast her as Cora?

CLEMENT.   We considered it. But she felt she wasn't right for it.

THOMPSON.   *(Smiling.)* Too old, perhaps?

MARGO.   I'll kill him.

CLEMENT.   *(Furious and icy.)* Age had nothing to do with it. It was a matter of — quality. But it would take me the rest of this broadcast to explain that to a layman like yourself. Even then you wouldn't understand.

THOMPSON.   I didn't know I was that dumb.

CLEMENT.   We live and learn, don't we? *(Margo applauds wildly.)*

THOMPSON.   Well, you were certainly lucky to find Miss Harrington. She must have made bags of money for you.

CLEMENT.   *(With an adroit snub.)* That's between me and my income tax collector.

THOMPSON.   I remember Miss Harrington made quite a sensation when she stepped into your wife's role in *The Golden Circle* one night. Was that why you chose her?

CLEMENT.   You could say it was a factor.

THOMPSON.   Then you might also say that Miss Harrington won this part strictly on her ability. Nobody pulled any strings?

CLEMENT.   Nobody pulls strings in my productions. Miss Harrington got the part strictly on merit. *(Karen lets out a staccato horse laugh.)*

THOMPSON.   Well, thank you, Mr. Howell. You've been very illuminating.... Now let's hear what the author of the play has to say. *(Clement and Lloyd change places.)* Ladies and Gentlemen, may I present to you one of the most *commercially* successful playwrights in America. Mr. Lloyd Roberts.

LLOYD.   Good evening, "Tally-Ho." That's a dubious introduction. I'd have preferred *artistically* successful.

THOMPSON.   Mr. Roberts, as the dramatist, you really had the final say in selecting Miss Harrington for Cora, didn't you?

LLOYD.   It was a mutual decision between Mr. Howell and myself.

THOMPSON.   Suppose there'd been a conflict? Suppose Mr. Howell had wanted Vera and you'd wanted Eve? You could still have forced the issue, couldn't you?

LLOYD.   It's my prerogative, yes. But it wasn't necessary in this case, so why bring it up?

THOMPSON.   I was curious. Without giving away any trade secrets, Mr. Roberts, would you tell our viewers why Mr. Howell withdrew from the direction of the play?

MARGO.   Because I put my little foot down, Bud.

LLOYD.   *(Thinking quickly.)* Who said he withdrew?

THOMPSON.   There was a strong rumor in the Sardi Set that he did.

LLOYD.   Surely you're too old a hand to pay any attention to that sort of gossip. *(Lying with conviction.)* There was never any question of Clement directing this particular show. It was agreed I should handle it when I sold him the play.

MARGO.   *(To Karen.)* I didn't know Lloyd was such a good liar.

KAREN.   *(Grimly.)* Darling, he's an expert.

THOMPSON.   One final thing, Mr. Roberts. To what do you attribute Miss Harrington's success?

LLOYD.   Eve is a marvelous example of how talent, hard work, drive and persistence pay off. She should be held up as an example to all young actors and actresses who are striving for success. She's never satisfied with her performance. She's continually struggling for perfection. That's always the mark of a great artist — from Bernhardt down to Margo Crane. *(Margo gets up and bows low to the TV set, then flops back on the sofa comically.)*

THOMPSON. Thank you, Mr. Roberts. And now I'm sure our viewers are dying to meet the young lady whose praises you have sung so highly. *(Eve comes forward and takes Lloyd's stool. Lloyd is about to resume his when Thompson stops him.)* Stay with us, Mr. Roberts. I'd like you both in the camera at the same time. *(Lloyd stands behind Eve.)* Ladies and Gentlemen, I have the honor to present Miss Eve Harrington.

EVE.   Good evening, Mr. Thompson. Good evening, everybody.

THOMPSON. We'll get right down to the business at hand. *(He takes the little box from his pocket.)* I have much pleasure, Eve, in awarding you the Thompson Medal for this season. It may seem an unimportant little item. You can't spend it or wear it or eat it. In fact, it's utterly useless. But it does stand for something. It means that you've given interviews when asked, that you've been polite and considerate to the Fourth Estate, and, most important of all, that when you've been asked a question by one of us press boys, you've given an honest answer. *(As he hands her the little box, Margo nearly chokes on her drink. Eve opens the box, and lifts out a little medal.)*

EVE.   Thank you, Mr. Thompson. I'll always cherish this. I realize how valuable the press are to my career. I intend to go on cooperating with them in the future.

THOMPSON.   I'm so glad to hear that, Eve. Because now I have a very personal question to ask you.

EVE.   *(All smiles.)* What's that, Mr. Thompson? Ask, I'll answer.

THOMPSON.   We had a tip this morning at the office. Some woman phoned in; said her name was Leila.

EVE.   Oh, she's my dresser.

THOMPSON.   She claims that the relationship between you and Mr. Roberts here is not entirely professional. Is there any truth to that? *(Margo sits up very straight and listens intently. Karen's face is a mask. Eve and Lloyd exchange embarrassed glances. Clement nearly falls off the stool.)*

EVE.   Forgive me, Mr. Thompson, but is that question quite ethical? Mr. Roberts is still a married man!

THOMPSON.   Still? But not for long?

LLOYD.   Since he's brought it up, Eve, you may as well tell him.

EVE.   *(To Lloyd.)* Well — if you don't mind.

LLOYD.   It'll come out in a day or two anyway.

EVE.   *(To Thompson.)* Well, since the cat's out of the bag, I'll be truthful. Mr. and Mrs. Roberts have been planning a divorce for some time. When he's free, Lloyd and I will marry. *(Margo jumps to her feet, quite sober, and switches off the TV. As she does so the lights on the R. of the stage go off, leaving the actors in the studio in darkness. The five of them disappear quietly into the wings during the following scene. They all take their stools, with the exception of Thompson, who leaves his where it is.)*

MARGO.   My God, Karen! Did you know?

KAREN.   *(Calmly.)* Of course. I've known for weeks what was going on.

MARGO.   You said he was an expert liar! Did you expect it to come out like this?

KAREN.   I wondered. That's why I put on mourning!

MARGO.   Now I understand all these drinks.

KAREN.   I know Eve. I'll bet you that the Leila who called the paper was really Eve, disguising her voice. Leila would never have done that. Eve wanted it to come out in public so that Lloyd would be securely hooked. She leaves nothing to chance.

MARGO.   Can't you prevent it?

KAREN.   What can a woman do when she's no longer exciting to her husband; when he falls in love with a younger woman who's full of beauty, talent, "honesty" and "integrity?" You let him go. You keep your pride — your lonely, miserable pride.

MARGO.   I'd fight. I'd use her own dirty methods too.

KAREN.   I tried that. That's why I had her investigated.

MARGO.   Did you show that report to Lloyd?

KAREN.   She outwitted me there too. She'd told him a lot of it in advance. God knows how she twisted it, but he believes her version. You can't reason with a man in love.

MARGO.   How did it all start?

KAREN. I think something subtly changed between us the night I made him apologize to you. Proximity to Eve did the rest.

MARGO. Now I'll tell *you* something. Do you know why I was so against Clement directing her? It wasn't because of the things she said about me. After "Tally-Ho's" awful column appeared, Clement told me that she'd made a pass at him when she wanted to understudy me.

KAREN. I wish you'd warned me. Well, it's too late now. She's got him. *(She pours out two drinks, finishing off the bottle.)* May I suggest we drink a toast to the second Mrs. Lloyd Roberts? So sweet — so simple — so innocent. May she trip over her bridal veil and break her neck. *(The two women drain their glasses. The lights black out. A moment or two later, Margo, who has slipped on her mink coat which covers her last dress, steps out of Karen's room and crosses down to the stool R.C., and sits on it. A spotlight picks her up.)*

MARGO. *(To the audience.)* Karen started this story with a prologue. In order to save her further embarrassment, I'll give you the epilogue.... Karen went to Sun Valley and got her divorce. The judge gave her a million dollars and the country house. All Lloyd got was the family cat. Eve and Lloyd were quickly married. Eve made two pictures on the coast. They were not very good. Just routine. That happens all the time in Hollywood. They buy a Broadway actress because she's unique and then don't know what to do with her. However, I think you will find in the future that her film career is going to pick up. There was a rumor printed in "Tally-Ho's" column last week — and you know what a first-class ferret he is — that all was not well in the Robertses' menage. Eve's constantly seen around town with a top-flight movie mogul. Can it be that love has worn off so soon? Is Lloyd just another stepping stone in the career of this talented young actress? Only time will tell. *(She points her finger upwards.)* But, believe me, Eve, you'd better stay up there on your starry pedestal. Because once you begin to slip, a lot of people will be eager to kick you on your way down. *(She gets off the stool, picks it up and starts to walk toward the stage door corner. She pauses for a moment.)* Oh — one final word. If any of you have daughters with stage ambitions, take my advice. Tell them — all about Eve. *(She continues on her way and disappears through the stage door. The curtain falls.)*

END OF PLAY

PROPERTY PLOT

ACT ONE

ONSTAGE:
Margo's Dressing Room
Dresses, on hangers
On dressing table:
   makeup things (cold cream, puffs, comb, etc.)
   whiskey bottle
   glasses
   ice bucket
   clock
   telephone
Highball glass (LLOYD)

Karen's Library
Coffee cups
Small nest of tables
On bar:
   telephone and telephone book
   assorted liquor bottles (including half-empty Scotch
      bottle for Act Two)
   ice bucket
   glasses
Cigarette box and lighter, on cocktail table

OFF LEFT:
Tray with silver coffee service and cups for 5

OFF RIGHT:
Tray of food (chicken pot pie, coffee) with napkin over it

PERSONAL:
Umbrella (KAREN)
Purse, with notebook and pencil in it (EVE)
Cigarettes and lighter (LLOYD)
Slip of paper (DELIVERY BOY)
Notebook and pencil (CLEMENT)
Cigar and lighter (CLEMENT)

ONSTAGE:
Downstage Area
Small table and chair
Play script, on table

ACT TWO

ONSTAGE:
Margo's Dressing Room
Sewing things (EVE)
Play script (LLOYD)
White stole, on hanger
Paper bag, with sandwiches and carton of milk
Suitcase
Purse, with script in it (EVE)
Highball glass (CLEMENT)

OFF LEFT:
Long mat cushions (2)
Tea tray, with crumpets
Muffin dish
Light coat and overnight case (MARGO)
Personal:
   wristwatch (LLOYD)
   notebook and pencil (THOMPSON)

ONSTAGE:
Margo's Dressing Room
Girdle (EVE)

Karen's Library
Book on cocktail table
Sheaf of official papers, in U.R. bookcase

OFF LEFT:
Garden chair
Garden scissors (KAREN)

OFF RIGHT:
Script (VERA)
Small table and chair
Ashtray, on table
Script (HARVEY)
Handbag, umbrella and script (EVE)
High stools (5)

PERSONAL:
Newspaper clipping (KAREN)
Wristwatch (KAREN)
Ten dollar bill (EVE)
Medal, in box (THOMPSON)
Cigarettes and matches (HARVEY)

SOUND EFFECTS

Applause (distant, closer)
Telephone ring

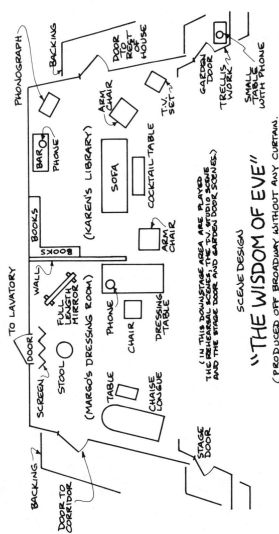